# Beyond Quality

# Beyond Quality

## An Agenda for Improving Manufacturing Capabilities in Developing Countries

Prepared for the
United Nations Industrial Development Organization

Steven R. Wilson, Robert Ballance and János Pogány

Edward Elgar

658.500917
W75b

Published by

Edward Elgar Publishing Limited
Gower House
Croft Road
Aldershot
Hants GU11 3HR
England

Edward Elgar Publishing Company
Old Post Road
Brookfield
Vermont 05036
USA

**British Library Cataloguing in Publication Data**
Wilson, Steven R.
    Beyond Quality: Agenda for Improving
    Manufacturing Capabilities in Developing
    Countries
    I. Title
    338.476091724

**Library of Congress Cataloguing in Publication Data**
Wilson, Steven R.
        Beyond quality: an agenda for improving manufacturing
    capabilities in developing countries / prepared for the United
    Nations Industrial Development Organization [by] Steven R. Wilson,
    Robert Ballance, and János Pogány.
        Includes bibliographical references and index.
        1. Developing countries—Manufactures—Management.  2. Industrial
    efficiency—Developing countries.  I. Ballance, Robert.
    II. Pogány, János.  III. United Nations Industrial Development
    Organization.  IV. Title.
    HD9738.D44W54    1995
    670'.68'5—dc20
                                                                        94–34105
                                                                        CIP

ISBN 1 85898 120 4

Printed in Great Britain at the University Press, Cambridge

# Contents

# Tables

# Figures

# Boxes

# Abbreviations

| | |
|---|---|
| CIF | continuous improvement firm |
| CIT | continuous improvement technology |
| EOQ | economic order quantity |
| FDI | foreign direct investment |
| FMC | focused manufacturing centres |
| FMS | flexible manufacturing systems |
| JIT | just-in-time manufacturing |
| LCL | lower control limit |
| MBO | management by objective |
| NUMMI | New United Motor Manufacturing Incorporated |
| PD | policy deployment |
| PDCA | plan-do-check-act cycle |
| QCC | quality control circle |
| QD | quality deployment |
| SMED | Single Minute Exchange of Dies |
| SPC | statistical process control |
| SQC | statistical quality control |
| TPM | total productive maintenance |
| TQC | total quality control |
| UCL | upper control limit |
| UNIDO | United Nations Industrial Development Organization |
| WIP | work-in-process |

# Foreword

Patterns of competitive advantage in world industry have changed dramatically over the past 20 years. Entirely new industries have emerged as older ones have died or become a mere shadow of their former selves. The forces driving these changes are a subject of paramount importance to anyone interested in the future of manufacturing. They include labour costs, capital investment, workers' skills and technological progress. Alongside these is another well-known ingredient of competitive success: the way these inputs are deployed and used depends on managers' skills and managerial techniques, and this, too, is a fundamental determinant of a firm's prosperity.

One of the key premises of this book is the suggestion that managerial techniques are becoming a more important determinant of competitive ability, and therefore deserve more attention than they sometimes receive. There are several reasons for this realignment among the forces that shape world industry. First, rapid advances in production technologies have led to many labour-saving innovations. The result has been to diminish the role of labour costs in the competitive equation. Second, the liberalization of capital markets and the large-scale movements of capital which have followed from this development are eliminating international differences in the cost and supply of this factor. Indeed, we expect to see a rise in foreign direct investment during the remainder of this decade and anticipate that an increasing portion of these funds will be directed to certain developing countries. Third, the world's markets for manufacturers are more turbulent and competitive than ever before and this places a premium on managerial capabilities. Finally, managerial techniques are evolving at an unprecedented pace, making the gap between 'state-of-the-art' management tools and more familiar methods greater than ever before. In tomorrow's world, it will be the way a factory is organized and managed that matters most in manufacturing.

The types of managerial techniques described in this book are neither fads nor untested ideas. In fact, their origin can be traced back to the 1940s in the United States of America. Shortly afterwards, these same ideas were exported to Japan where they were improved, elaborated and further refined over the next 40 years. Today, they have been adopted — in full or in part — by a number of firms around the world. Our fear, however, is that this international migration of managerial principles and techniques is too selective. Manufacturers in industrialized countries are proving to be willing converts but in developing countries the pace of acceptance is far too slow.

The managerial techniques which are the subject of attention here are known as *kaizen* to the Japanese and are generally referred to as 'methods of continuous improvement' in other countries. The United Nations Industrial Development Organization (UNIDO) has been active in this field for several years. The goals of the Organization are to assist firms, industries and governments in developing countries in mastering these techniques and to accelerate their diffusion throughout the manufacturing sector. UNIDO's work in the area of continuous improvement is part of a wider-ranging programme which includes assistance in meeting international standards, elements of total quality management and total quality control. The experience accumulated through these programmes demonstrates how effective these methods are, and serves as a primary source for much of the material on which this book is based.

MAURICIO DE MARIA Y CAMPOS
*Director-General*

# Explanatory Notes

The following classification of economic groupings is used in the text, and in most tables, in conformity with that used by the Statistical Office of the United Nations Secretariat: 'developing countries' includes all countries, territories, cities and areas in Africa (except South Africa), Latin America, East Asia (except Japan), South Asia and West Asia (except Israel); 'industrialized countries' includes Northern America (Canada and the United States of America), Europe, Australia, Israel, Japan, New Zealand and South Africa.

Unless otherwise indicated, 'manufacturing' includes the industry groups listed under Major Division 3 in *Indexes to the International Standard Industrial Classification of All Economic Activities* (United Nations publication, Sales No. E.71.XVII.8).

Mention of commercial enterprises does not imply endorsement of those enterprises by the United Nations.

Dates divided by a dash (1970–75) indicate the full period involved, including the beginning and end years. References to dollars ($) are to United States dollars, unless otherwise stated. References to tons are to metric tons, unless otherwise specified.

Annual rates of growth or change are based on data for each year throughout the period indicated and are calculated using a semi-logarithmic regression over time, unless otherwise specified.

# Acknowledgements

The United Nations Industrial Development Organization (UNIDO) has been active in the related fields of quality control, statistical process control and standardization for a number of years. This book draws heavily on UNIDO's experience in these areas. The contribution of others — academics and researchers, UNIDO's field staff and managers of manufacturing plants in developing countries — is also acknowledged. Dr. Richard Sanders and Dr. Mary Leitnacker of the Management Development Center at the University of Tennessee served as consultants on statistical quality control, providing much of the data and analysis appearing in Chapter 5 and the Statistical Appendix. Others who supplied material and data include Mark Sabau of Packard Electric International (Mexican Division), Dr. Nicholas Phillips, Director of Engineering and Technology for Elamex S.A. and Paul Hesp and Masayoshi Matsushita of UNIDO. Dr. Antonio Bós kindly shared the results of his own research in this field. Finally, Marcia Gordon-Leiter, Theresa Traun and Brigitte Leutner of UNIDO assisted in the research and preparation of the manuscript.

This publication has been prepared by Steve Wilson, Robert Ballance and János Pogány who are responsible for the views and opinions expressed therein. These views and opinions do not necessarily represent those of other persons or institutions mentioned here.

# 1. Continuous Improvement in Changing Markets

Recent years have brought more than the usual amount of reorganization and reappraisal in world industry. Coming after a prolonged period of uninterrupted growth, this development represented a dramatic reversal in fortunes. Manufacturing had thrived for several decades and by the beginning of the 1970s the world's landscape was cluttered with multinationals and other huge firms, most of them based in industrialized countries. Subsequent years have not been kind to these industrial giants. Some are now a shadow of their former selves and a few have disappeared entirely. Commentators tell us that the reason has usually been a failure to adapt to changing circumstances. That diagnosis is probably accurate but it is also too general to suggest many remedies.

One of the premises on which this book is based is that today's markets for manufactures are quite different from those existing in earlier years. Such a distinction is not original. The same point has been stressed by economists, business consultants and policy makers. However, opinions differ about the reasons for this change. Some analysts argue that the volatility which exists today is much greater than ever before, while others suggest that internationalization of markets, the accelerated pace of technological progress or some other phenomenon is the culprit.

Whatever the interpretation, several of the macroeconomic and microeconomic forces that lie behind these changes are easy to identify. The world economy grew at an unprecedented rate between 1950 and the early 1970s (Madison, 1982), but in more recent years growth has been erratic, wreaking havoc with investment plans, macroeconomic policies and international economic relationships. Other sources of volatility are policy-induced. Wide swings in exchange rates, the liberalization of capital markets and the large-scale movements of capital which accompany these circumstances are examples. Meanwhile, the intensity of international competition has been growing. Firms are constantly reducing the time required for product development and accelerating the pace of technological progress in other ways. Consumers also contribute to these circumstances. Patterns of consumption are changing as households grow richer. A significant minority of consumers are prepared to pay more for some version of a product which is unique, more luxurious or better serves their particular needs. As customerization grows in importance, markets fragment and producers struggle to satisfy a diverse set of consumer preferences.

The volatility in today's markets is so pervasive as to cast doubt on some of the principles that guided companies in more peaceful times. One prominent victim may be the manufacturer's incessant search for economies of scale. According to traditional thinking, firms must produce in very large quantities in order to reduce their unit costs. Each batch of items could number thousands or tens of thousands. With production runs of such immense size, it is difficult for the firm to respond to a sudden shift in competitive conditions or consumers' preferences. The search for greater economies of scale and related goals may not be such a prominent feature of manufacturers' plans in the future (see Box 1.1).

Other manufacturing guidelines are less well known, but equally suspect in the new market environment. Some examples are the organizational structure of large firms, their methods of collecting and using in-plant data and their dependence on inspection as a means of quality control. Each of these subjects is examined in later chapters. For the present, it is sufficient to note that many companies are turning away from traditional principles.

The alternative forms of organization and work procedures that are gaining favour have evolved over many years. Some methods can trace their origins to the 1920s in the United States. Later, these ideas were exported to Japan where they were improved, elaborated and further developed. By the 1980s firms outside Japan had begun to experiment with the new methods. Today, they are being adopted — in full or in part — by a large number of the world's manufacturers. Our fear, however, is that this international migration of managerial principles and production techniques is too selective. Firms in industrialized countries are proving to be willing converts but in developing countries the pace of acceptance is far too slow.

There are many determinants of a firm's competitive position. Those discussed in this book are only part of a longer list which includes well-known factors like the cost of labour and capital, workers' skills, technologies and public policy. But in our view, some of these traditional factors are not as important as they once were. The changing pattern of competitive advantage is no longer being driven by cheap labour and low wages. Nor will capital investment, however large, ensure that a firm thrives in today's markets. In contrast, methods of management, the organization of production lines and the shop-floor procedures which are employed are more important than in the past. The way a factory is organized and operates matters most in this emerging age of manufacturing.

## Box 1.1 Contrasting views of manufacturing efficiency

Closely related to the idea of scale economies is the concept of 'economic order quantity' (EOQ). The measure, which indicates the optimum number of items in a run or batch size, can refer to a single machine or an entire production line. In either case, it is determined by two cost components. The first is 'carrying costs' which consists of interest charges on unfinished pieces and materials, along with charges for wages and rents to store these inventories and move them around the factory. Set-up charges are the other component and include the costs of preparing the machine or production line to produce a particular item, along with the cost of test samples and any other preliminary steps. The carrying costs per unit of output rise as the batch size increases but set-up charges decline. Adding the two components together gives a measure of production costs which first declines and then rises. The minimum point on the total-cost curve is the EOQ (see Box Figure 1.1).

The EOQ is a well-known part of the mass producer's arsenal of cost controls but its usefulness is being seriously challenged. One criticism is that the EOQ results in production runs which are too large in today's fast-changing markets. Another is that set-up and carrying costs are not the only determinants of batch size. Other activities that are not isolated by conventional accounting practices also contribute to costs. Examples are the amount of wasted time and materials which occur during manufacturing, the motivation and skills of the workers and the quality of a product. Finally, critics argue that very little can be done to reduce carrying costs whatever the amount, but a great deal can be done to reduce set-up charges and the more nebulous costs referred to here. Arguments such as these are winning over many managers, leading them to modify (or even discard) traditional guidelines like the EOQ in order to compete in today's turbulent markets.

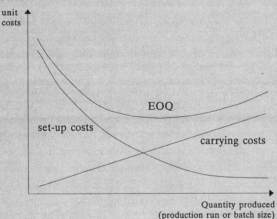

There is no shortage of new ideas on how firms should deal with the matters in today's fast-changing markets. However, many of these ideas have proven to be little more than fads and others have not fulfilled their promise. The techniques and principles discussed in this book have a longer history and have proven to be extremely effective in improving productivity and competitive prowess. Moreover, they have been successfully employed in different parts of the world and in a wide range of industries. Known as *kaizen* in Japan, these techniques are referred to in this book as 'methods of continuous improvement'.[1] Later in this chapter we describe the objectives and principles on which these methods are based, along with the areas of application which receive the most emphasis. But before turning to the microeconomic matters which are the heart of this book, it is useful to consider how these concepts are transferred across national boundaries since this issue is especially relevant to the discussion which follows.

## MECHANISMS FOR INTERNATIONAL TRANSFER

Long experience has shown that international trade and foreign direct investment (FDI) are the most effective means of transmitting new ideas and technologies around the world. Companies may voluntarily join this process by selling their products abroad, investing in foreign markets or establishing tie-ups with other producers, either in their home market or abroad. Those that abstain soon fall behind in the race to survive. Most will find themselves competing against imports or facing competition from local rivals that are foreign-owned or work in partnership with foreign collaborators.

Though trade and FDI are alternative mechanisms for entering the world economy, they have distinctly different implications for the firm. Expanded trade entails few inter-firm linkages. And the linkages which are created tend to be rather superficial in nature. A different set of circumstances applies to FDI. Production-based links tend to be rather complex, requiring close working relationships between the foreign investor and local partners. The issues which investment-related linkages pose involve companies' organizational structure, managerial methods and production procedures. In other words, they are precisely the types of issues which concern us in this book.

Trade has traditionally been the more important route to world markets. The growth of world trade from the 1950s until the early 1970s surpassed all expectations. Though it continues to expand at a steady pace, trade's preeminence is being challenged by foreign investment. For example, statisticians estimate that the value of the total stock of foreign investment is around $2,000 billion — equivalent to about one-third of all the world's private productive assets. The turnover generated by these assets in 1992 was bigger than total world exports. Experts go on to speculate that FDI may only be in its 'take-off phase', perhaps in a position comparable to world trade in the 1950s (see, for example, Julius, 1990).

The pattern of FDI is also expected to change. At present, most FDI is between industrialized countries but a wider dispersion of capital flows is already emerging. The commitment by many developing countries to greater education, market liberalization and privatization is beginning to pay off with stronger economic growth and a growing number of middle-class consumers. By the end of the decade, the average return on FDI could be much closer to the high rates of the 1960s than the modest ones of the 1980s.[2] This is part of the reason why experts predict that the real value of FDI going into developing countries in the year 2000 could be two to three times greater than in 1990.

The developing countries that gain most from this surge in foreign investment will not necessarily be those attracting the greatest amount of FDI. Large inflows of foreign investment sometimes lead to correspondingly large amounts of imports which is not the ideal result. To maximize the benefits of FDI, local manufacturers should be able to supply the newcomers with materials, components, semi-finished products and services. In other words, the foreign-owned firm should have strong links with the local economy, generating not only jobs or additional exports but boosting domestic demand for raw materials and intermediate inputs. This objective — to ensure that foreign investment generates business links with local firms — suits the preferences of many investors today. International companies are accustomed to working closely with a wide range of subcontractors and independent suppliers in their home market and would consider similar arrangements in their foreign factories.[3] In fact, the possibility of 'local sourcing' is becoming a more important determinant of FDI as the significance of other criteria wanes (see Box 1.2).

Foreign investment is growing in importance and is gradually drawing more and more firms into the international orbit. If developing countries are to make the most of these opportunities, their firms must meet the same managerial and organizational standards as their manufacturers in the industrialized world. Companies that are experienced practitioners of continuous improvement will have a distinct advantage. They have a much better chance of attracting foreign capital or — equally important — supplying these foreign-owned firms with the inputs they require. On these grounds, public officials and managers of private firms should both have a strong interest in programmes of continuous improvement.

In conclusion, the claims we make in support of continuous improvement go far beyond the benefits accruing through FDI. Much more significant gains can be realized in terms of customer satisfaction, higher productivity, capital

**Box 1.2    The changing criteria for FDI**

Every investment is unique, though changes in the relative importance of general investment criteria can be identified. For example, simple types of investment incentives such as tax holidays are no longer of much significance. Large companies acknowledge that if these incentives are the main reason for investing in a particular country it will be wiser to look elsewhere. Another traditional magnet for FDI — cheap labour — is also losing its appeal owing to the growing sophistication of global organizations and modern methods of production. Meanwhile, big investors display a growing interest in procuring local inputs. Their preference stems from a combination of concerns which includes timely delivery of defect-free inputs and materials at competitive prices and other attributes of continuous improvement.

It is difficult to gauge the extent to which foreign-owned firms rely on imports rather than local suppliers although recent data from Mexico sheds some light on this issue. That country's assembly or maquiladora industry has been a magnet for foreign investment. By several standards the experiment can be judged a success. For example, over 2,100 maquiladora plants are in operation and the sector is presently Mexico's second largest earner of foreign exchange. However, only about 5 per cent of the product inputs used in the maquiladoras are actually purchased from Mexican suppliers (Brannon, James and Lucker, 1990). Recent surveys have shown that many managers would prefer that a greater portion of their inputs come from local sources. In some instances no local source of supply exists but where local alternatives are available they are not regarded as competitive because of their quality, price or erratic supply schedules (Wilson, 1992).

savings, waste reduction and other forms of efficiency. The way these goals can be achieved through continuous improvement is the overriding theme of this book.

## WHAT IS CONTINUOUS IMPROVEMENT?

Continuous improvement refers to a firm's unceasing efforts to upgrade products, manufacturing processes and other parts of its production system in order to meet customers' requirements while concurrently reducing inefficiency and costs (see Cole and Mogab, 1994).

Two general points follow directly from this brief definition. First, change is the leitmotif of continuous improvement. Such an approach may seem to be a curious one for a manufacturing firm to adopt; people generally prefer to work in a stable and predictable environment. However, a firm's ability to adapt to the volatile conditions that prevail in today's markets requires that workers and production methods be extremely flexible. Second, the firm's quest for ways to improve poses a special challenge to managers. They have to create an environment which will convert the learning and experience of the workforce into a steady stream of improvements. But they can only succeed with the full cooperation of others — in particular, the shop-floor workers who are the company's real 'value-adders'. Managers must strike a balance between their traditional role of 'controlling from above' and a new one which requires 'consent', or at least a more consensual approach.

Continuous improvement proceeds through a constant stream of alterations or adaptations in a firm's production processes, decision-making practices and organizational methods. Some will have widespread repercussions and may require facilitating investments. The vast majority, however, are tiny, costless modifications and it is their cumulative effect which is the true source of competitive strength. It follows that most improvements will not be obvious to the outsider until they come together in some dramatic and obvious innovation such as just-in-time manufacturing (JIT).

Practitioners of continuous improvement can also be distinguished in terms of the great emphasis they place on upgrading workers' skills and abilities. The standard view of the 'learning curve' assumes that a fixed and externally developed technology is introduced into the firm through investment. Learning then becomes a rote process as the firm strives to maximize efficiency with the use of outside technology (see Schramm, 1994). In contrast, continuous improvement proceeds through a series of endogenous advances that relies on experimental learning within the firm. This is a creative process which works best when personnel have a general perspective and understand how their tasks and responsibilities fit with other undertakings in the plant.

Firms can not pursue the goals of continuous improvement without tinkering with each minute part of their production system. In doing so, they may choose from a wide range of techniques and procedures. Some are used to monitor manufacturing processes to ensure efficiency and precision; others are intended to improve specific parts of the manufacturing system such as inventory control or maintenance routines. By making use of these tools, the successful user of continuous improvement will progress along its own technological path with changes emerging from the very production processes of the firm.

An exhaustive account of all the tools and options available to the continuous improvement firm (CIF) is not possible here. In the interest of brevity, we have chosen to emphasize certain methods and fields of application rather than others. The main considerations which have guided our selection of subject matter are the following:

- We focus on the ways techniques of continuous improvement can be employed on the shop floor. These same methods can also be applied in other activities, ranging from research and development to the distribution of finished products. However, new practitioners will generally record the largest and quickest gains by concentrating on shop-floor applications. That emphasis is also consistent with orientation of most firms in developing countries, since the manufacture and assembly of products overshadows their involvement in research or distribution.

• One of our primary goals is to demonstrate how a carefully implemented programme of continuous improvement can yield substantial cost savings and productivity gains while still reducing the rate of product defects.

• Not all techniques of continuous improvement are equally suitable for every firm. Some will be most appropriate for the beginning practitioner and it is these which receive the greatest emphasis. Other methods are best employed by firms having several years of experience with continuous improvement and are described in less detail.

These lines of emphasis narrow the focus of discussion but the list of topics to be considered is still a long one. Many deal with particular areas for improvement such as maintenance, plant layout, machinery design, methods of handling materials, means of sharing information and related matters. Alongside these specific applications are several more general ones which are intended to help the firm monitor and control its production system and the manufacturing processes which make up that system. The latter are statistical in character and are usually the first phase in any programme of continuous improvement. The statistical principles on which these procedures are based are explained in the following section.

**Coping with Variation in Manufacturing Processes**

Manufacturers must constantly deal with a complex set of interactions involving materials and parts, production processes and technologies, and workers and managers. No two bits of material are the same, no two machines perform identically and no two operators are equal in skill, dedication and powers of concentration. This interaction between materials, machinery and people is inevitable. But it is also a source of variation which must be brought under control before a firm can introduce any lasting improvements in its production system.

One simple example of variation occurs when a manufactured article departs in some way from pre-determined standards. Another is observed when two items are manufactured in exactly the same way but turn out somewhat differently. In either case, it is statistical variation that explains the discrepancy between the actual and desired outcome. Such deviations occur in all manufacturing processes but serious problems arise if the difference between the actual and desired outcome is significant. When variation is large or unpredictable, the firm's ability to anticipate future outcomes is undermined. A manager is no longer able to plan production or to forecast costs and revenues. Equally damaging is the fact that large or unpredictable amounts of variation push up production costs or result in significant customer dissatisfaction.

To illustrate, suppose the manufacturer of a granular product experiences high and unpredictable variation. The firm can not predict with any certainty the average amount of its product which will be available in each container. Sometimes this amount exceeds the weight specified on the container label, while at other times it is lower. Customers will be dissatisfied if they receive less than the amount stated on the label. To avoid this outcome, the manufacturer sets an unnecessarily high limit on the amount of granular material that is dispensed per container. This correction prevents shortfalls but it also results in wasteful overfilling and increased costs. By reducing variation, the producer would be able to lower the fill-weight target and cut costs without risking customer dissatisfaction.

Savings of this kind can be identified through standard accounting and financial practices.[4] Other benefits are less obvious, however, and may escape the attention of accountants or financial analysts. A reduction in statistical variation can lead to fewer inspections, simplified routines and less time for the rework of defective items. With these improvements, a firm should be able to scale back its inventories of work-in-process and take advantage of other opportunities. For example, as the amount of variation in the production system is reduced, it becomes easier to meet customers' specific requirements or to raise the quality of a product or service. The result is a larger number of return buyers (often bringing new customers), greater sales and a stronger competitive position. Benefits such as these typically escape the attention of the accountant.

Firms that embark on programmes of continuous improvement begin by distinguishing between two fundamentally different types of variation:

- *Common-cause variation* arises from sources common to the entire system. These disturbances are due to flaws in the production system and will persist without fundamental improvements in specific production processes.

- *Special causes* of variation occur at isolated times or locations. Unlike common causes, they affect only certain parts of a production system and are not necessarily repeated.

By observing the pattern of statistical variation over a sufficiently long period of time, we can distinguish between common and special causes. A manufacturing process that is subject only to common-cause variation is described as being stable or 'in control'. In such a case the same level of variation prevails over time and the proportion of defective outcomes can be predicted. When both common and special causes are at work, the amount of variation is not predictable and production processes are unstable or 'out of control'. Importantly, all special causes of variation must be removed before management turns to the real problems: continuous improvements can not begin until a process is stable, or in control.

A simple illustration of the two sources of variation is found in Figure 1.1. Observations for process A show month-to-month changes in labour productivity. The latest observation is less than the previous one, although it falls within the boundaries of the historical series. Because these boundaries appear to be constant over time, we attribute the variation to a common set of causes within the existing system. The situation is different for process B. Month-to-month changes are comparatively small but the most recent value lies well outside the historical pattern. This result implies that process B is unstable. Managers should be able to identify the reasons (or special causes) for the unusual deterioration and remove them. However, neither process A nor B represents an ideal condition. Special causes must be removed before comprehensive methods for continuous improvement can begin. All processes and production systems (including those which are in control) need improvement.

Casual observers tend to attribute unanticipated outcomes to special rather than common causes. This bias reflects a deeply ingrained belief that mistakes such as defects, cost-overruns, accidents or poor service result from the poor performance of individuals or similar unusual events (see Box 1.3). Such misinterpretations occur when managers are unclear about the statistical stability of their manufacturing system. In fact, experts believe that more than 90 per cent of all problems and opportunities for improvement are inherent to the system (Deming, 1986, p. 315). In other words, variation is typically due to common rather than special causes but the onlooker often assumes otherwise.

## Organization and Highlights

The following chapter describes the main advantages of continuous improvement for manufacturers in developing countries. Later chapters deal with organizational implications for the firm, the implementation of actual procedures and the experiences of specific companies that have employed these techniques. Below, we provide a summary of the highlights and main points discussed in subsequent chapters.

*Figure 1.1    Stable and unstable production processes: an illustration*

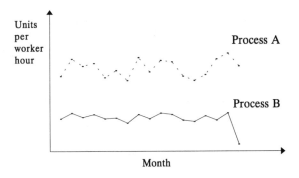

**Applicability for developing countries**
Programmes for continuous improvement are a familiar part of the manufacturing scene in industrialized countries but can they be equally effective for
manufacturers in developing countries?  Chapter 2 deals with this question,
advancing several reasons why continuous improvement is particularly suitable for use in this part of the world.

The economies of most developing countries are characterized by an
abundance of cheap labour and a relative scarcity of capital. These conditions
are similar to those faced by Japanese manufacturers shortly after the Second
World War.  Like many of their counterparts in today's developing countries,
Japanese companies lacked the finances needed to purchase new equipment
and modernize their plants. Engineers and managers quickly recognized that
continuous improvement was an effective and inexpensive way to counter
these drawbacks. Product quality could be improved and costs reduced without
large-scale spending for additional equipment and machinery.

The opportunities which these methods offer in terms of capital savings are
discussed in some detail in Chapter 2.  They include: a reduction in the down-
time required for repair and maintenance, a speedier process of machine
changeover so firms can shift quickly from production of one product model
to another, the possibility of increasing plant capacity without additional capital
injections, and the option of incorporating new technologies in existing
machinery rather than purchasing the latest versions.  Striking examples where
firms using continuous improvement have been able to operate more efficiently
than competitors with newer and more sophisticated machinery are noted.

A second important attribute is the high priority a CIF places on the effective
use of its workforce. More conventional manufacturers — for example, those

---

**Box 1.3    Biased assertions about the cause of defective goods or services**

Many people will instantly assume that lost airline baggage is due to 'lazy or incompetent' workers, that an automobile recall is evidence of 'shoddy workmanship', or that poor restaurant service is the result of 'rude and surly waiters'. Few pause to consider that the airline might be spacing flights too closely; that management of the automobile firm might have endorsed a faulty design, accepted the lowest bidder for parts, or rushed production in order to maximize output. Similarly, waiters may be overworked and have little control over critical variables which affect the quality of service (for example, the performance of cooks, the quality of food obtained from vendors or the work schedule). More generally, the poor quality of a consumer good or service is usually attributed to the lax performance of an individual or cultural 'work ethics' and the like. The production system and the managers who bear ultimate responsibility for such a system escape blame.

---

relying on the principles of mass production — also pay attention to the performance of the workers. However, they tend to use large amounts of capital relative to labour and it is natural that they are mainly concerned about maximizing the efficiency of capital.[5] The CIF can be distinguished from the mass manufacturer by its emphasis on improving the efficiency of both capital and labour with the latter receiving an especially high priority. This orientation is more compatible with social and economic conditions in developing countries where labour is abundant and unemployment is high.

Other advantages include a greater measure of flexibility and the opportunity to engage in endogenous forms of improvement. One goal of continuous improvement is to enable firms to produce different product mixes in small batches and still operate profitably. These 'economies of flexibility' can mean the difference between success and failure for companies in developing countries where markets are small and subject to erratic shifts. The matter of endogenous progress is no less important. Most production technologies are perfected in the industrialized world and therefore reflect the cost structure in those countries. The results are not always appropriate for use in the developing countries. Successful implementors of continuous improvement will be able to generate their own innovations and adapt equipment to suit their own unique conditions.

**Using informal types of production data**
Most large companies are organized according to the principles of mass production. These methods offer significant advantages to the manufacturer but they also have constraints. One is the mass manufacturer's limited ability to gather and use certain types of production information (see Bós, 1991).

Every firm generates large amounts of production information. Some is quantitative in character and is regularly collected by all manufacturers, large and small. Other kinds of production-related data are not so easily compiled or interpreted. The latter may refer to a relatively complicated situation or require intimate knowledge of a particular manufacturing process. Such data is known as 'informal information' to distinguish it from the more conventional sorts of quantitative measures. Informal information is generated during the daily course of events on the factory floor. It is derived from the experiences of production-line workers and pertains to the use of materials, components, machinery and the manufacturing processes of the firm.

Mass manufacturers have elaborate methods to collect formal information. They use this data for several purposes: to monitor the performance of machinery and workers, to plan production schedules and determine output strategies or to identify and rectify problems in the manufacturing system. The same firms are less adept at handling informal data. They have difficulty collecting such information and presenting it to managers in a form which facilitates decisions. The mass producer's organizational structure, its hierarchical form of decision-making and the high degree of specialization it imposes with regard to job responsibilities and workers' functions all inhibit the effective use of informal data. An inability to utilize shop-floor data is a severe handicap whenever companies seek to improve their products or manufacturing systems. Yet this process of rejuvenation and modernization is not only essential but must occur with increasing frequency as competition intensifies. Lacking complete information about conditions on the shop-floor, a manufacturer's efforts to improve performance and efficiency will often go awry.

A related distinction between the CIF and the mass producer results from the way each firm views the fundamental concepts of time and efficiency. The mass producer will generally try to achieve greater 'economies of time' which means that it seeks to produce a given volume of output in a minimum amount of time. Job responsibilities, the arrangement of machinery on the factory floor and the division of labour between managers and workers are all designed to accelerate the pace of work. The CIF is also concerned with the use of time but assigns a high priority to other factors as well. It distinguishes between costs generated by production-line activities and those attributable to manufacturing overheads (for example, costs associated with inventories, inspection procedures and machine changeover). Studies of large manufacturing establishments have found that the costs of overheads are frequently as much as twice that of workers on the production line. The CIF is constantly searching for ways to reduce these overheads.

The indicators and yardsticks each type of firm uses to measure efficiency are consistent with their differing orientations. Because the mass producer is concerned with formal data and optimum use of production time, it relies heavily on indicators such as estimates of productivity per labour hour or machine output per hour. These same measures are important to the CIF but others are also common. One such measure which is discussed in Chapter 3 is known as 'process-throughput efficiency'. The concept is defined as the amount of time materials and inputs are actually being worked on, divided by the total amount of time they spend in the manufacturing system. Studies conducted in industrialized countries have found that it is not uncommon for materials and inputs to be manipulated or worked on as little as 1–2 per cent of the time spent in the factory. Conversely, the time which workers must devote to overhead activities is high.

**Tools of continuous improvement**
A number of techniques for continuous improvement are discussed in Chapter 4. Some are too sophisticated for firms that have just embarked on such a programme, just as others will be too elementary for the experienced practitioner. The appropriate mix will change as a firm gains competence, and between these two extremes is a wide range of choices where experience and judgement are the main guides. Moreover, each firm will constantly modify and refine the methods it employs until they suit the user's specific needs.

One theme which recurs throughout this chapter is the need for careful and extensive planning before launching each new phase of a programme. Scientific methods of investigation should be employed to identify bottlenecks and sources of inefficiency or waste. These routines emphasize the need for preparatory steps — planning, testing (preferably on a small scale), checking and verification of results — before new steps in a production process are permanently altered. Experienced companies may no longer acknowledge their reliance on such simple techniques although the way they organize improvement efforts still owes much to their earlier mastery of these principles.

The emphasis placed on simplifying production methods, satisfying customers' needs and coordinating all aspects of continuous improvement is illustrated by some of the techniques outlined in Chapter 4. All manufacturers need some mechanism to determine their buyers' preferences. The notion of 'quality deployment' enables firms to stay in touch with their market and tailor their products to meet customers' requirements. A system of 'policy deployment' can be set up to ensure that decisions filter down through the ranks and that all workers understand the reasoning behind these decisions. The idea of improvement teams, the advantages and disadvantages of quality control circles and systems of 'total productive maintenance' are among the other techniques described in Chapter 4.

All this planning and coordination requires that managers and workers determine those parts of the manufacturing system which contribute to costs but add nothing to the value of the finished product. Some of the techniques explained in this chapter can be used to identify these problems. Likely sources of waste and inefficiency are scattered throughout the factory. All too often, they are accepted as part of the normal routine, especially in mass production firms which rely on inspection-bound manufacturing systems. Examples include excessive inventories, variation in production processes which requires rework or results in defectives, unnecessary waiting time by workers or machines, or excessive movements of materials around the plant. These and other problems are prime targets for improvement procedures.

**Monitoring and controlling manufacturing processes**
The efforts of a firm to improve its competitive position must be coordinated to ensure that the more important problems receive the most attention and that all changes are carried out in an effective manner. A crucial part of this work is the statistical analysis described in Chapter 5. The discussion is aimed at readers with little or no statistical training. The main purpose is to describe in simple terms how these statistical methods are applied and what they should accomplish.

Statistical process control (SPC) has a role to play in any manufacturing environment — even if the firm is not fully committed to the goals of continuous improvement. Unfortunately, the benefits derived from these statistical tools will be limited in such a case. No statistical methods, however powerful, can take the place of managers who constantly assume responsibility for making improvements in their firm's operations. But when used as part of a disciplined and sustained programme, SPC can provide managers, engineers and line supervisors with the insight and knowledge necessary to make improvements.

SPC offers several advantages which make it particularly attractive to manufacturers in developing countries. Most important, it provides a means of improving productivity and product quality without incurring large additional expenses for equipment and machinery. Second, manufacturers in industrialized countries are thoroughly familiar with SPC and want their suppliers and subcontractors to be equally experienced. When foreign manufacturers set up plants in developing countries, they expect that local suppliers meet the same standards. Finally, the firm that adopts SPC has some measure of flexibility in the way it employs these tools; the statistical principles are invariant but the criteria and methods of application can be altered to suit local conditions and circumstances.

SPC has an especially important role to play during the early stages of continuous improvement, though its prominence should diminish over time. The statistical analysis will supply managers with the information they need to eliminate special causes of variation and take the necessary steps to ensure that these disturbances do not recur. Once this phase has been completed, common causes of variation will have been identified and gradually reduced. The manufacturing system may have been overhauled and products redesigned, but the need to monitor each production process should eventually become unnecessary. The charts and graphs which were so much in evidence during the early stages of continuous improvement can then be dismantled. Unfortunately, this degree of proficiency is not always achieved. Many firms that introduce these statistical programmes never succeed in eliminating common-cause variation. The statistical apparatus becomes a permanent feature of their operations. In that capacity, it represents the graphical counterpart of a human inspector, serving merely as insurance against a loss of control.

One of the main reasons for difficulties during the early stages of continuous improvement is that senior management are not actively involved in the programme. This attitude is soon transmitted to the workforce. Many employees assume that the charts and production methods are just another form of work appraisal with the hidden purpose of eliminating jobs or wringing more from each employee. Another frequent source of problems is the inability of the firm to make maximum use of on-site information. This weakness can mean the firm becomes 'stuck' in the early stages of SPC while its better-organized competitors move on to more sophisticated forms of continuous improvement.

### Continuous improvement in action

UNIDO's efforts to promote continuous improvement have produced a large body of evidence based on the experiences of firms in developing countries and transition economies. Chapter 6 draws on this information. Several of the firms discussed there were participants in UNIDO-sponsored programmes. In other instances, the firms themselves initiated these programmes independently, with UNIDO staff participating as observers.

The companies singled out for attention have very little in common aside from their emphasis on continuous improvement. They are located in different parts of the world (Africa, Central Europe, Mexico and the Caribbean), they range from beginners to experienced practitioners, they operate in different industries and serve a diverse set of customers. This heterogeneity is intentional; the fact that such a dissimilar group of companies can all benefit from these methods illustrates the general applicability of continuous improvement.

One of the points stressed in Chapter 6 is that success is not limited to certain types of firms or ways of doing business. Most of the techniques are simple and straightforward, while the emphasis on cooperation and information exchange has an appeal that is general. Another is that the biggest savings and improvements in efficiency are to be found on the shop floor. Furthermore, these opportunities are not limited to the larger and richer firms. Small or even tiny firms are capable of using many of these techniques; in fact, their natural emphasis on teamwork and the closeness of management to production can give them an advantage over larger rivals.

There are some qualifications to our thesis that continuous improvement has a general applicability. Small firms, for example, may not be able to afford all the training their workers require. One option is for them to band together and work closely with local training institutes. Government support will also be essential, and for this to occur, policy makers must be convinced that continuous improvement holds benefits for a large portion of the manufacturing sector. Valuable support can also be provided by international organizations, multinationals and other big investors in the country.

## Obstacles and opportunities

Several of the more formidable barriers encountered when implementing programmes of continuous improvement are 'internal' to the firm, involving the attitudes of managers, workers or both. Managers' misconceptions about continuous improvement are the most common source of difficulties. Some expect near-instant results while others assume that particular procedures such as statistical process control are synonymous with the overall approach. Firms that embark on a programme of continuous improvement with these presumptions will be disappointed. Another frequent source of difficulty arises when senior managers delegate responsibility for improvement programmes to subordinates, either because they do not regard these activities as sufficiently important or because they lack a comprehensive understanding of the work.

More widespread opposition emerges when managers use improvement programmes as a means of shedding workers. Such an approach is common, although it runs counter to the goals of continuous improvement. Procedures for sharing information and various forms of cooperation are jeopardized when concerns about job security are intermingled with efforts to improve productivity and efficiency. If possible, any necessary reductions in the workforce should be distinct from improvement efforts and be completed before the latter programmes are launched.

Firms in developing countries must either locate competent managers to run their improvement programmes or find ways to train the necessary people. Unfortunately, there are few reliable sources of such managerial expertise in these countries. State-owned firms and family firms are unlikely training grounds. Multinationals can be a useful source of training and experience in improvement activities. However, a number of these firms are reluctant to hire locals and some have even discontinued improvement procedures that are standard practice at headquarters.

The question of how culture influences managerial style is a recurrent one and enters into this discussion in a narrow sense. We reject the suggestion that continuous improvement is appropriate for some cultures and not others. The performance of workers and managers is determined by the organizational environment in which they work rather than by cultural traits. Managerial style, however, is a product of the individual's culture and is relevant in this specific context. The drawbacks of ascriptive and paternalistic managerial styles are discussed in Chapter 7. Although both approaches are much in evidence in developing countries, the same is true in Japan and other Asian economies where continuous improvement has thrived. Neither of these managerial styles offers a healthy setting for improvement programmes, but with small adaptations the conflicts should not be great. In any case, methods of continuous improvement may be more suitable to certain cultures than are many of the organizational tools for mass production such as performance appraisals, management by objective and highly specialized forms of training and work procedures.

Having examined the main obstacles to improvement programmes, attention turns to issues of public policy, education and on-the-job training. Based on UNIDO's own experience, one of the most effective means of promoting the widespread dissemination of continuous improvement technologies is to establish permanent centres for this discipline. If affiliated with a university, the centre can employ faculty members on a part-time basis and use those facilities. External funding would be required during the start-up phase (usually for 2–3 years), but the operation should eventually become self-financing as with similar institutions in industrialized countries.

The advantages of a permanent facility are several. Customized courses can be developed for specific industries and firms which take into account special needs and local conditions. A more effective balance between theory and practical application can be realized by relying on universities or consultants to provide all training. Faculty in the centre are expected to provide on-site advice and assistance by helping to implement and monitor newly introduced methods of continuous improvement. A long-term presence is crucial since the time needed for a firm to become an experienced user of continuous improvement is lengthy. Finally, permanent institutions are able to establish lasting links with industry and trade associations and with chambers of commerce. Such links are an effective means of promoting continuous improvement but are rarely present when other groups — for example, universities or consulting firms — serve as the main conduit for training and dissemination.

In conclusion, the advantages offered by continuous improvement are numerous and the costs justified. Manufacturers in developing countries can benefit immensely by mastering these techniques. The task is not an easy one, but with support from policy makers and international institutions, the goal of widespread dissemination can be achieved.

# NOTES

1.  We use the term continuous improvement because it best describes the main strength of this approach. Other terms used to describe similar methods and principles of manufacturing include: lean manufacturing, total quality management, world class manufacturing, flexible manufacturing and best-practice manufacturing.
2.  Not all countries and regions of the world are active participants in this investment-driven climate. Certain developing regions and parts of the national economy will fare much better than others. One indication of this fact is that the growth of FDI has been accompanied by a shift in sectoral priorities. Investment going into services and high-technology manufacturing is destined mainly for industrialized countries, while in developing countries the emphasis is on basic manufacturing and natural resources.
3.  Many multinationals traditionally followed practices that discouraged links with local suppliers. Prominent examples are the use of different types of transfer-pricing schemes and the creation of captive subsidiaries. These practices continue today but as issues of quality and improvement assume greater importance as their popularity wanes.
4.  However, such financial and accounting practices can also provide a deceptive picture of the health of an organization. If standards incorporate high variability, processes are said to be 'on budget', even though there is significant waste. More importantly, possible financial gains due to increased operating efficiency and continuous improvement are often difficult to understand in the context of standard accounting and financial practices and may be overlooked (see Reeve, 1991, pp. 403–27).
5.  The priorities of the mass manufacturer are implicit in the tools it uses to evaluate the performance of each factor of production. The performance of workers is measured by rough-and-ready indicators such as output per worker hour. In contrast, a wide array of financial and accounting tools are employed in the acquisition and operation of machinery and equipment. Similarly, if a manager of one of these firms squanders time, money or equipment, he will be held accountable. Yet he will have few means of judging workers' performance except according to the amount they produce.

# 2. Continuous Improvement Technologies for Developing Countries

Are the technologies of continuous improvement well suited for use in developing countries? We believe they have wide applicability in this part of the world and outline our reasons here. The chapter begins by describing what we mean by a technology and then goes on to discuss the advantages that continuous improvement technologies offer manufacturers in developing countries.

## CONTINUOUS IMPROVEMENT AND OTHER FORMS OF TECHNOLOGY

In popular terms, technology is frequently regarded as being embodied in various tools, in different types of sophisticated machinery or in complex products like computers or jet aircraft. Such a description may lead to the mistaken assumption that new technologies can be purchased 'off the shelf' and then installed in plants. In practice, the acquisition of new technologies is not that simple. Machinery which has been designed and developed in the industrialized world is typically meant to operate under economic conditions which prevail in those countries. The same equipment and procedures could be inappropriate for use in many developing countries where a different set of economic conditions exist. Lacking the necessary know-how and detailed knowledge, the purchasing firm may be unable to adapt its new equipment to local conditions.

A second difficulty with the populist view is the tendency to ignore technologies that are not closely identified with objects or equipment. Broader definitions exist in the scientific literature where both tangible and intangible forms of innovation and progress are described. Important examples of intangible technology include: the principles by which a firm is managed, organized and operated, various methods of developing workers' skills and knowledge, and alternative approaches to decision-making. Production gains or improvements in efficiency that are derived from the application of these techniques are just as valuable as those attributed to the successful introduction of modern equipment. These intangibles are legitimate forms of technology and their effectiveness should be judged in relation to other alternatives.[1]

The distinction between the scientific and popular definitions of the term can be best illustrated with an example. Toyota's development of the revolutionary production method known as 'Single Minute Exchange of Dies' (SMED) represented a technological innovation for the automobile industry. In the popular view, the physical tools which characterize this system might be regarded as the real technological breakthrough. Such a description would be misleading, however, since it ignores all the incremental improvements and advances which made SMED possible. The tools themselves are the outcome of a process that took years to complete and was driven by technologies of continuous improvement (see Box 2.1).

It follows that any assessment of a plant's technological capacity may be erroneous if it is based solely on the availability of the most sophisticated types of capital equipment. Again, an example drawn from the experience of Toyota illustrates the danger. In the mid-1980s, the company's number 9 Kamigo engine plant was recognized as the world's most efficient (Schonberger, 1986, Chapter 4). Surprisingly, that plant was equipped with American-made machinery which was 20 years old. Comparable plants in the United States had much newer and more sophisticated machinery and, by popular definition, employed more 'advanced technology' than the Toyota plant. Toyota's superior performance is explained not by the availability of modern equipment but by the rigorous application of continuous improvement technology (CIT). Managers, maintenance workers and line operators collaborated to improve

---

**Box 2.1   Accelerated machinery changeover: an example of CIT in action**

As Japanese automobile makers grew in size, certain costs rose exponentially. One solution was to reduce the changeover times for machinery so that different models could be produced efficiently in smaller batches. Single Minute Exchange of Dies (SMED) is based on the distinction between 'external' and 'internal' set-up activities. External activities are performed while a machine is operating. For example, transporting old dies to storage is an external operation, while mounting the dies is an internal set-up activity. Methods of continuous improvement were used to convert internal into external activities. The configuration of dies had to be altered, but SMED did not require any new machinery. Eventually, manufacturers cut the time required for die changeovers from several hours to a few minutes. Other benefits were: reduced inventories, more efficient use of plant space and smoother scheduling with suppliers. The implementation of just-in-time (JIT) techniques of inventory control depends on this move to more flexible forms of production.

every phase of the production line, from the arrangement of machines to maintenance schedules, elimination of machine down-time and so on. Thus, it was the use of CIT rather than the effectiveness of physical tools which determined the plant's superior performance.[2]

In conclusion, the interpretation of technology we employ extends beyond tangible tools to encompass intangible forms of innovation and progress. While the effectiveness of physical tools may depreciate over time, the intangibles described here may actually gain in potency. Methods of continuous improvement fall into the latter category, representing a set of options that can be used in conjunction with (or in place of) other forms of technological progress. The following section considers some of the major benefits which continuous improvement offers manufacturers in developing countries.

## ADVANTAGES FOR DEVELOPING COUNTRIES

Most descriptions of continuous improvement have focused on applications in industrialized countries. However, the important message of this chapter is that similar techniques can be effectively used in developing countries. The discussion stresses several characteristics:

- The pattern of industrial growth in most developing countries tends to be capital-intensive. This orientation is questionable, given the abundance of cheap labour in these countries. CITs offer a different set of options which, if efficiently implemented, can lead to improvements in labour productivity, products and processes.

- Various elements of CIT offer opportunities for capital savings that would not be realized through alternative forms of technical progress.

- CITs allow the manufacturer greater flexibility than most other technologies. For example, production systems can be readily adapted to changing economic and technical conditions, the product mix can be quickly altered and the volume of production which is necessary for the firm to break even is reduced.

- Continuous improvement is primarily an endogenous form of progress. Managers and workers of the firm are the driving force for most improvements. This orientation ensures that the production system is gradually tailored to suit the firm's needs and the local environment.

## Human Effort and Labour Productivity

The economies of most developing countries are characterized by an abundance of labour and a scarcity of capital. It follows that labour tends to be relatively cheap while capital is more expensive. CITs place an especially high priority on the effective use of people, making them more suitable in these conditions than other, relatively capital-intensive forms of technological progress.[3]

The expense of sophisticated technologies has not deterred manufacturers from pursuing this option. There are a number of reasons for their preference. Acquisition of the most advanced capital equipment is sometimes regarded as a prerequisite for modernization and expansion. Industrialists may assume this is the quickest way to boost productivity and ensure that local plants are competitive in domestic and international markets. They have support from some economists and businessmen who reject development strategies that advocate more extensive use of labour. The latter group argues that workers' performance can never match state-of-the-art technologies embodied in modern machinery or that labour is overpriced and unproductive (see Box 2.2).

The industrialist's bias in favour of capital-intensive methods of production is occasionally supported by policy makers. The relative cost advantage of labour can be undermined by policy decisions which significantly reduce the price of capital (for example, through direct or indirect subsidies for the purchase of equipment and machinery). Manufacturers then find it cheaper to expand or modernize their plants by acquiring very sophisticated forms of capital equipment rather than using older technologies and hiring additional workers. In extreme cases, firms will actually purchase new machinery and

---

**Box 2.2    People and machines: a managerial double standard?**

Firms typically employ different standards to evaluate the performance of machinery and workers. A wide array of financial and accounting tools are used to help managers decide which machines to buy and how they should be used. If a manager squanders money or equipment, there are numerous standards by which he is held accountable. However, the same firms may judge workers' performance in very crude terms according to the amount they produce. The successful manager is one who gets 'more out of workers'. He may push employees to work harder, faster and longer or use greater amounts of unskilled, cheap labour. Whatever the case, opportunities for increased productivity are lost when the improvement potential of workers is overlooked. Such practices are just as wasteful as the poor utilization of capital investment. This explains why many plants including some with the most modern and latest equipment have had to close their doors.

release workers — in other words, they 'substitute' capital for labour even though there is an abundance of the latter.

The literature on this subject is wide-ranging but a majority of analysts are critical of investment programmes and industrial policies which encourage extreme forms of capital intensity or the substitution of capital for workers (see, for example, Colman and Nixson, 1985, pp. 372–91). Some regard the importation of sophisticated machinery as undesirable because maintenance is expensive and requires skills that are rarely available locally.[4] Others note that such equipment is designed to operate with long production runs which are not suitable in the small markets of developing countries. A third criticism is that extensive reliance on advanced forms of capital equipment is neither economically nor socially desirable in countries where unemployment is high. In such conditions it is preferable to make maximum use of the more abundant and cheaper resource (labour) by substituting it for the scarcer, more expensive resource (capital).

A singular emphasis on capital-intensive forms of modernization and growth has obvious drawbacks. CITs can help to rectify this imbalance, but are they a practical alternative for firms in developing countries? There is empirical evidence to suggest they are. Many developing countries have made significant strides in raising literacy rates and producing well-trained engineers and technicians. This pool of skilled and semi-skilled workers can provide the nucleus for a continuous improvement process. All workers will require training in CITs, but there is ample evidence to show that even employees with limited job experience and only a primary education are capable of handling these methods.[5]

The manager's goal in a programme of continuous improvement is to enhance and capitalize on the skills, experience and creativity of all those working in the firm.[6] When information is shared and barriers between job functions are eliminated, analytical tools like SPC can supply valuable insights about the way different parts of the manufacturing operation relate to the whole. A dedicated workforce can then ensure that improvement is a long-term goal, leading to reduced costs, greater throughput and higher quality. Improvement activities are part of the daily routine and entail no 'opportunity cost' in the sense of production losses. Such an orientation stands in contrast to more traditional methods which presume that increased efficiency is realized by using people and machines more intensively or by introducing new capital equipment.

Detailed evidence gathered from the experience of firms in developing countries is encouraging. Among manufacturers engaged in assembly-type operations, some of the most significant improvements have been realized when workers were allowed more responsibility and personal control over the work area. Machinery, tools and materials were rearranged in ways that better suited the tasks being performed. Operations such as moving, storing, packing and unpacking containers and counting items were all streamlined. Modifications like these led to a much smoother flow of production through the plant. Other benefits included: less physical exertion, fewer work-related injuries, greater job satisfaction and lower rates of employee absenteeism and turnover (see Box 2.3). Nor did managers report problems when implementing some of the more complex forms of continuous improvement. With training, workers having only a primary education were sufficiently proficient in data collection, maintenance of control charts and other aspects of SPC.[7] Employees often worked within teams that began by discussing and analysing the importance of variation in manufacturing processes. Afterwards, they were encouraged to identify and implement process improvements in their respective work areas (Wilson, 1992).

Improvements achieved by these assembly operators were obviously simple in scope and made use of inexpensive tools and materials that would be available in any developing country. The results nevertheless had the predictable effect of reducing the use of materials, inventories and work-in-process and eliminating certain types of rework and repair. Managers reported that in some cases the improvements were so cost-effective that they were introduced in other plants located in the United States or Europe.

When attention turns from processing operations to more traditional forms of manufacturing, the evidence is less abundant but no less encouraging. Manufacturers in Zimbabwe have employed methods of continuous improvement to improve productivity and eliminate defects. Similar results are reported for various industries in other developing countries. They include: electronics-related manufacturers in India (Kaplinsky, 1993, pp. 19–26),

---

**Box 2.3   Employee responsibilities and employee turnover**

Rates of employee turnover are a chronic problem in the assembly and manufacturing industries of many developing countries, often running as high as five to ten per cent per month. Ironically, managers who regard high rates of employee turnover as inevitable are often the first to introduce measures which perpetuate the problem. They devise very simple and repetitive tasks for entry-level workers which require no training or previous experience. New employees are then hired off the street and given no responsibilities except to follow instructions. Much lower rates of employee turnover are reported by firms that train their entry-level employees and allow them a degree of responsibility. The latter employees learn more about their jobs and can contribute to a programme of continuous improvement.

metalworking plants in Brazil (Ruas, 1993, pp. 27–33), Brazilian automobile and electronics plants (Bós, 1991), the Brazilian footwear industry (Ruas, 1989 and Piccinini, 1990) and automobile manufacturers in Mexico (Ramirez, 1993, pp. 58–64). The precise nature of the improvements varies from one industry to the next but the overall gains are nevertheless impressive.

## Opportunities for Capital Savings

Firms that successfully implement CITs should find that their capital requirements are less than would otherwise be the case. These savings may be partially offset by additional spending in other areas but the net benefits could still be significant.[8] Important examples of capital-saving opportunities include:

- A longer and more productive life for existing machinery, coupled with improved performance due to less down-time for repair and maintenance.

- The possibility of increasing plant capacity without additional capital infusions.

- More extensive reliance on used rather than new capital equipment.

The productive life and performance of capital can be extended in two ways. One method, which is discussed in some detail in Chapter 4, is known as total productive maintenance (TPM). Because TPM assigns primary responsibility for maintenance to machine operators rather than specialized workers, it can be carried out on a continuous basis. While operators must be trained, the benefits of TPM are fewer equipment failures and reduced machine down-time for repairs.[9] Ideally, a piece of equipment should perform as well or better near the end of its productive life than when it was first purchased (Rodriguez, 1992, pp. 152–53).

Continual adaptation and modification of existing machinery are other ways to extend its productive life. A smoother and more efficient flow of work through the plant can often be attained by altering the layout and usage of machinery. Such moves require that the machinery itself be modified. Over time, further modifications are made to accommodate new conditions and operating circumstances. The eventual result should be a distinctive combination of equipment and machinery that is especially suited to the firm's requirements. Once this point is reached, the machinery is much like some form of proprietary technology which can provide a competitive edge over rivals. Because the modifications are usually simple and inexpensive, this method can be more attractive than outright purchase of expensive new equipment.

The impact of TPM and various methods for equipment modification can be inferred from patterns of capital spending in different parts of the world. In Japan, where preventive maintenance and CITs have a long history, about 60 per cent of all capital expenditures are to upgrade the capabilities of existing equipment and manufacturing processes. Meanwhile, innumerable modifications of equipment have culminated in the development of various 'mistake-proof' devices that are crucial to the efficiency of Japanese plants (Shingo, 1986). The expenditure pattern in the United States is quite different, in part because TPM and programmes for equipment modification have only recently become accepted practice. The bulk of capital spending among firms in that country has gone into additional capacity or replacement of existing machinery (Hayes, Wheelwright and Clark, 1988).

The second possibility, that CITs can increase a firm's production capacity without additional capital infusions, has been argued by Cole, Mogab and Sanders (1992). To illustrate, assume that two firms have the same cost structure and produce two products which consumers regard as being about the same. Both have been using methods of mass production with long production runs, but one (firm 'A') begins to incorporate CITs. Incremental improvements become part of the firm's day-to-day operations. Managers, engineers and operators work together to determine ways of reducing variation within the production system. Soon, activities which do not add value to the product can be eliminated. The costs associated with inventories, storage, inspection, rework and scrap all begin to fall. Eventually, firm A's output capability is enlarged although the same amounts of resources, machinery, labour, materials and energy are being used. It not only enjoys lower unit costs than firm B, but now has the capacity to satisfy any extra demand realized through improvements in product quality and/or lower prices.

A third potential source of capital savings is the ability to make efficient use of machinery and capital equipment which is not state-of-the-art. This option has its critics. Decisions about technologies and equipment are often made by a firm's engineering and technical staff who follow the latest innovations and understandably favour 'cutting-edge' technologies. Much stronger objections are voiced by a small group of industrialists and analysts. Some suspect that suppliers of used equipment are intent on ridding themselves of unwanted and obsolete machinery. Others fear that extensive reliance on used equipment will prolong a state of technological backwardness. Critics go on to argue that firms relying on used equipment have no access to support services (for example, training, warranties, repair and maintenance) and may not be able to manufacture products which meet high standards for performance and quality (see Box 2.4). Government officials who subscribe to any of these views will frequently advocate policies to discourage the purchase or importation of used machinery.

Concerns such as these are valid in certain instances, but every decision to exclude all but the latest generation of technology and equipment should be justifiable on economic grounds. Instead, they are often based on considerations that are not purely economic. Nor do critics take into account the role of continuous improvement. The example of Toyota's Kamigo plant illustrates that methods of maintenance and operation can be a more important determinant of competitive abilities than the technology which the equipment embodies. Through a long-term process of incremental improvement, the workforce redesigned the physical plant so that it served the firm's needs better than the newer equipment in competitors' factories.

Aside from the technological issues involved, most analysts agree that older equipment has certain practical disadvantages: it requires frequent maintenance and generally has a shorter productive life than newer versions. However, firms that employ CITs are better able to cope with these problems than their competitors. First, maintenance operations are part of the daily routine. Responsibilities are assigned in a way which limits the costs of maintenance while extending the lifetime of equipment. Second, a 'hands-on' approach to maintenance provides workers many opportunities to learn about the equipment and its mechanical processes. That knowledge feeds back into the improvement programme, paying dividends over the longer term. Third, 'post-acquisition' alterations are relatively easy since the latest technological innovations are not already engineered into the equipment (James, 1974).[10]

---

**Box 2.4    Is second-hand equipment an efficient option?**

The issue of whether to purchase second-hand or modern equipment can only be resolved on a case-by-case basis. First, critics who argue that the use of yesterday's technologies will jeopardize product quality are sometimes correct. Yet there is a vast range of products which can be profitably manufactured with less sophisticated technologies. In the latter case efficient maintenance practices can be a more important determinant of a plant's performance than the vintage of its equipment. Second, new equipment often comes with guarantees and a package of services not offered to purchasers of used equipment, but that practice has drawbacks as well as advantages. The buyer of new equipment pays for these services in one way or another and may then be locked into a dependent relationship with the vendor. Finally, there is no data to suggest that second-hand equipment is being 'unloaded' on developing countries. Evidence from the United States shows that all but a small fraction of used equipment which changed hands was sold inside the country (James, 1974, p. 134). Supporting evidence comes from a survey of over 100 foreign subsidiaries operating in Mexico. Many used equipment which was older than that found in plants located at the headquarters. When the capital vintage differed, it was the Mexican plants that generally had higher levels of productivity and quality (Wilson, 1992).

In our opinion, arguments favouring the use of machinery which is not state-of-the-art can be persuasive. Unfortunately, the bulk of experience with this option has been accumulated by firms that made no use of CITs. A very large proportion are assembly-type operations which have combined the cheap labour of developing countries with older, mature technologies. Their competitive abilities depend mainly on low-paid workers who perform simple, routine tasks. Most these assembly plants follow the classic principles of mass production: their systems are geared to minimize costs for a given product and process and their investment in the local economy is modest. Such factories are described as 'footloose' operations; when wages rise (for whatever reason), the firms simply relocate to another low-wage country.

Not surprisingly, the outcome has been criticized as failing to promote broad-based growth and self-sustaining development (see Sklair, 1990). This experience has shaped most opinions about the use of second-hand equipment. However, the footloose firms we describe here have a very tenuous relationship with the host economy. Cheap labour is their only source of competitive strength and when that advantage is eroded they relocate. This relationship is in marked contrast to that of firms making use of CITs. The latter will necessarily have a strong commitment to training and development of workers' skills. Those talents are used to make existing technologies 'more dynamic' and to adapt them to suit the local environment. Soon, competitive advantage depends not on low wages but on the in-house skills the firms have nurtured. Companies that apply the methods of continuous improvement therefore have an anchor in the local economy and will not willingly move elsewhere when wages begin to rise.[11]

**Flexibility in Developing Markets**

Because continuous improvement depends on a process of constant change, it provides a degree of flexibility that other technological alternatives lack. This flexibility can be achieved in various ways.

First, the firm requires that managers and workers gain experience in a wider range of functions than would be true for manufacturers organized to produce in a mass-production mode. Because the workforce acquires a good understanding of most manufacturing processes, people are better able to respond to unforeseen problems and can make an effective contribution to the programmes of improvement. Second, the layout of the production line is designed to minimize the time needed to alter the product mix or adjust the level of output. Machines are arranged and operated in ways that maximize throughput and keep idle time to a minimum. Third, costs are reduced by systematically monitoring all activities and eliminating those that do not add value to the product. The firm constantly strives to cut back and eliminate inventories, storage areas, rework, repair and inspection. Similar efforts are made to avoid waste and duplication. All such activities lead to lower production costs per unit of product.

Programmes such as these have several goals, all of which will lead to greater flexibility of the firm. One is obviously to reduce costs. Another is to create a 'leaner' or simpler form of production by eliminating those steps or operations which limit the firm's ability to respond quickly to new conditions. A third way of achieving greater flexibility is the rapid changeover from one configuration of machines and workers to another. Different product mixes require different combinations of machinery and workers. Through the use of CITs, the firm can produce various mixes of products in smaller batches and still operate profitably.[12] This phenomenon has been termed the 'economies of flexibility' (Cole, Mogab and Sanders, 1992). Though other technological alternatives also claim to provide greater flexibility, these options are quite different from those offered by continuous improvement (see Box 2.5).

Greater flexibility enables the firm to avoid some pitfalls encountered by manufacturers operating according to the principles of mass production. That method assumes an entirely different economic environment which can absorb high volumes of throughput and long production runs. Such conditions are necessary in order to drive down unit costs and attain the scale economies needed for efficient operation. Unfortunately, markets in many developing countries are too small to absorb these large volumes of output.

Manufacturers employing methods of continuous improvement should have a wider range of economically viable options from which to choose. They are better able to tailor their production mix and output levels to changing

---

**Box 2.5    Contrasting forms of flexibility in manufacturing**

Many writers refer to flexible forms of manufacturing in terms similar to those used to describe CIT. Others associate the term with the idea of a 'flexible manufacturing system' (FMS) which is operated by numerically-controlled machine tools that work under the guidance of central computers. There is some evidence to suggest that FMS is not as flexible as expected, unless it is combined with other techniques such as continuous improvement. For example, a comparative study of FMS operations in the United States and Japan reports an 'astonishing lack of flexibility' among the former firms. In the United States the average number of parts made by FMS was 10 compared to 93 in Japan. American firms apparently used FMS to produce a few parts in large volumes rather than making a variety of parts at low unit costs. This difference in approach is attributed to the more extensive Japanese experience with the manufacturing processes, their emphasis on organizational learning and similar attributes of continuous improvement (Jaikumar, 1986).

conditions in the local market. In its most advanced form, the use of CITs will combine the specialist advantages of small-job shops with the scale advantages of high-volume production (Best, 1990).

## Endogenous Improvement and Cultural Adaptation

Firms that successfully implement CITs will generate their own innovations and improvements. Managers may borrow promising ideas and techniques from elsewhere but these are soon assimilated and adapted to the firm's particular circumstances. Progress depends mainly on the effort and creativity of managers and workers. The local culture, working through the attitudes, decisions and customs of the employees, exerts a strong influence on the firm's overall pattern of innovation and technical progress.

The precise role played by cultural forces is impossible to identify when attention focuses on individual firms or industries. More can be said if we adopt a much broader perspective. The system of mass production, for example, was developed and perfected to serve the growing markets of industrialized countries. Key features of that system include: extensive forms of specialization, well-defined types of hierarchical management, an emphasis on company-wide planning, performance incentives and competition between individuals. These practices have been effective because they depend on a set of values and behavioural norms with deep cultural and historical roots in the industrialized world.

Methods of continuous improvement are clearly based on a different set of principles and values, where cooperation and coordination are at least as important as competition between individuals and the company's chain of command. In fact, many of the values and behavioural norms that are an integral part of the mass production system could be superfluous to a firm which opts for CITs (see Box 2.6). Developing countries with value systems that are in no way compatible with the principles of mass production could turn cultural biases to their advantage by considering alternative ways to organize production.[13]

The role of culture may also explain some of the problems western managers have experienced in implementing CITs. Most of the tools and technologies on which this approach depends are meant to be used in a general, system-wide context. Instead, managers sometimes employ techniques such as SPC to resolve very specific issues — for example, to analyse elements of a particular manufacturing process or to find a short-term solution to a problem. Applications such as these reflect the prevalent western belief that by perfecting individual pieces, the whole can be made perfect. Such an orientation is implicit in the organization of many mass production firms. Departments, machines, workers and managers are dedicated to specific and specialized

**Box 2.6    The suitability of quality programmes in different cultures**

Expatriate managers have reported that implementation of CIT is often easier to accomplish in a developing country than at home. One reason is that local engineers and workers have no experience with other methods of organizing production and will accept CIT without reservations. Another is that labour unions in some industrialized countries will frequently depict programmes for quality and improvement in a negative way, fearing that layoffs will result. This interpretation can be reflected in workers' attitudes. Third, many workers in developing countries are comfortable with systems which embrace characteristics such as group identification and respect for experience. CIT capitalizes on these values by its emphasis on cooperation and coordination between groups of people.

Western managers sometimes find the accompanying forms of behaviour (for example, the avoidance of individual recognition apart from the group) irrational but their assessment tends to overlook basic cultural realities. Workers in many developing countries rarely find anything strange about the absence of individual ratings and rewards that are so common in firms organized according to the principles of mass production. That attitude seems to be supported by statistical evidence. Such ratings can be arbitrary and will often be met or exceeded due to chance. Even when it can be statistically demonstrated that one person's performance is superior to others, invidious recognition can actually dampen overall improvement (Aguayo, 1990).

tasks; if each part of the firm operates efficiently, the organization as a whole is expected to function smoothly.

A more holistic point of view can be found in Japan where the entirety of the enterprise tends to be seen as qualitatively different from the sum of its individual parts (Yoshida, 1989). In other words, the competency of individual components does not ensure that the enterprise will thrive. Based on observations such as these, analysts have hypothesized that one reason for the success of programmes of continuous improvement in Japan may be that the commitment to mass production is not so deeply entrenched as elsewhere (Matsushita, 1988). The fact that these attitudes are similar to those displayed in many developing countries suggests that the same methods could also be suitable there.

## NOTES

1. Hibbard and Hosticka (1982) state this view succinctly when they note that the common organizational form of a pyramidal bureaucracy is as much a technology as the word-processors, microcomputers, filing systems and calculators that are so essential to the work of the organization.
2. For other evidence citing similar results, see Shingo (1986).

3. Firms that successfully implement CIT regard people rather than machinery as the main source of innovation and improvement. Toyota's Director of Production Control has argued that 'too much automation can backfire .... If it's too complicated, workers are intimidated'. Ultimately, even a flexible automated system will be of less significance than a dedicated workforce which continually improves quality through suggestions and study (Jagawa, quoted in Miller, Woodruff and Peterson, 1992, p. 37).

4. Sellers of advanced equipment sometimes lock buyers into an expensive package of maintenance and repair services. Contracts stipulate that only trained technicians employed by the vendor will be allowed to work on machinery. Any upgrading or modifications must also be performed by the vendor's technicians. Such a package of services diminishes the possibilities of 'hands-on' learning by workers and engineers in the buyer firm.

5. There is a growing body of literature which demonstrates that workers in developing countries with low levels of skill and education can be trained to use CIT efficiently. For a discussion of such practices in metal manufacturing enterprises in Zimbabwe, see Posthuma (1993); in electronics manufacturing in Tanzania see UNIDO (1993); in Indian auto components manufacturing and electrical products manufacturing, see Kaplinsky (1993) and for manufacturing enterprises in Brazil, see Fleury (1993).

6. The following is a typical view of management in the continuous improvement firm: 'Matsushita makes people before making products .... Of all the resources that are necessary to run a corporation, I believe that the human factor is the most important. It is no exaggeration to say that the quality of a company is determined by the people who staff it. No matter how well organized it may look on paper or no matter how advanced its management techniques are, a corporation will not prosper unless its managers and employees can effectively use the organization or techniques. The same is true of capital, plant and equipment, or materials.' (Konosuke Matsushita, in UNIDO, 1993, p. 41).

7. Curiously, the interest in training programmes for quality and improvement tends to be higher among production-line workers in developing countries than managers. Managers often resist the introduction of new techniques and organization methods (Posthuma, 1993; Fleury and Humphrey, 1992; Wilson, 1992). In some cases the 'quality' programmes they implement are really meant to increase the intensity or pace of work without putting in place a sustained system of improvement (Franzoi and Rodrigues, 1993; Ruas, 1993).

8. CIT is not expensive in terms of its capital requirements but it requires proper training in key areas such as process and product improvement, cost and design. These investments can yield substantial returns and should be seen as akin to outlays for new equipment rather than as a sunken cost or expense. Ironically, many firms that would not consider cost savings via reduction in machine maintenance will readily cut worker and management training.

9. TPM also stretches the time between repairs and therefore reduces the firm's outlays for replacement parts.

10. Many workers and engineers in developing countries may be more skilled in these activities than their counterparts in industrialized countries. They have considerable experience keeping old machines running despite a shortage of parts and little money. The urban informal sector in most developing countries includes large numbers of small-scale maintenance and repair shops, all of them employing informally-trained or self-taught mechanics. An impressive variety of innovative activity occurs in these shops, even in the poorest of surroundings. Such creativeness would be invaluable in a disciplined programme of TPM and can be used to maintain and adapt older machinery.

11. The scenario we describe is reminiscent of circumstances in Japan in the early 1950s. Manufacturing at that time relied on cheap labour and used capital sparingly. The many firms that embraced quality control and the early elements of CIT did not relocate when wages later began to rise (see Deming, 1986). In fact, very few set up any overseas operations until they had become huge corporations which were converted into multinationals.

12. The ability to maintain product quality and control costs, yet produce in small batches rather than long production runs, should be an extremely profitable accomplishment for small and medium-sized firms. It is these companies that serve as subcontractors, assemblers and suppliers for the large national and multinational firms operating in developing countries. The market represented

by these large companies is not being exploited by small and medium-sized firms. In Mexico, for example, the large manufacturers and exporters in the maquiladora sector buy less than five per cent of their inputs from Mexican suppliers. Many managers would prefer local sources of supply but can not because of problems with quality and availability (see Wilson, 1992). Similar findings are reported in Brazil (Bós, 1991).

13. The role played by culture in the process of economic development has been of considerable interest to economists. Some have argued that certain cultures found in the developing world embrace value systems which would be inimical to a process of industrialization based on the principles of mass production (Myrdal, 1968).

# 3. Organizational Structures and Information Flows

Most large manufacturers throughout the world have organized themselves to operate according to the principles of mass production. All such firms aim to minimize their costs through long production runs which can be sold in big or rapidly expanding consumer markets. Other distinguishing characteristics include: heavy investments in plant and equipment (which imply high fixed costs), production of a limited number of product versions or models to avoid frequent changeover in machinery and production lines, highly specialized job assignments and a hierarchical structure that divides the company into several discrete divisions or departments. Using principles such as these, the modern-day version of a mass manufacturer has attained a size and scale of production which far exceeds that of its predecessors.

The production capabilities of these firms have increased many fold, though their organizational and structural characteristics have changed very little (Best, 1990). At the same time, drastic changes in the global marketplace have created new challenges for mass producers everywhere. Some of these developments were noted in Chapter 1 but two deserve special mention here. First, firms now operate in a more competitive and uncertain environment than ever before. Second, manufacturers are under incessant pressure to ensure that their products and processes meet new, and usually higher standards. The forces creating these changes originate from several different sources. They include: more discriminating customers, more flexible competitors, more stringent regulations and more influential interest groups. No company, however powerful, can ignore their significance.

Circumstances such as these place a premium on a firm's ability to identify new directions of change and to respond swiftly. Managers of mass production firms are acutely aware of the challenges they face. Mergers and acquisitions, rationalization of capacity, massive layoffs and countless other corporate strategies are all part of their response. Nor have they hesitated to 'borrow' production methods and new techniques from competitors and firms in other industries. The search for a winning combination of products and production processes is wide-ranging, but all too frequently the results have been disappointing.

Recipes for success in today's more competitive environment defy generalization, although a few common themes can be identified. One of these, the use of production-related information, is discussed here. This subject is important for two reasons. First, firms must have a complete and comprehensive view of how their production systems function before they can respond effectively to competitive threats or otherwise improve their existing operation. Manufacturers that lack the necessary production information are unlikely to choose an appropriate course of action. Second, the route by which information moves through an organization reveals a great deal about how the firm works. Information tends to move along the path of least resistance and its course will disclose decision-making channels that do not appear on any organizational chart.

Manufacturing enterprises generate vast amounts of production-specific data. Much of this is quantitative in character and is obtained through the sort of routine measurement exercises that are carried out by virtually all firms. Another type of production information is informal in character and is possessed by on-site workers. Such data is generated during the daily course of events on the factory floor. It deals with various kinds of problems and experiences relating to the use of materials, machinery and other production-line operations. Casual observers may assume that this informal information is of minor significance but in reality it is an essential input if the firm is to realize the costless and highly effective types of improvement described in Chapters 1 and 2.

By focusing on the ways production information is collected and used, we can highlight differences in organizational form. At one extreme is the 'continuous improvement firm' (CIF) which attaches great importance to both informal and quantitative sources of information. At the other is the mass production firm where greater emphasis is placed on more formal, quantitative types of data. In practice, the differences between these two organizational entities may not be as great as the following discussion implies; the sharp contrasts we draw are partly for expository purposes.

The discussion begins by examining how production information moves through a firm organized to operate according to methods of mass production. Attention then turns to information flows in an enterprise dedicated to continuous improvement. Our purpose is to demonstrate how each firm makes use of available data to improve its production processes. An important distinction between the two firms' approaches is in their interpretation of efficiency and process time. This subject is discussed in the concluding section of the chapter.

# INFORMATION FLOWS IN MASS PRODUCTION FIRMS

Procedures for gathering and processing production information are deter-mined in part by the degree of specialization which the mass production firm imposes (see Bós, 1991). Such specialization has its roots in early twentieth-century ideas about 'scientific management' and can be observed in the way managers and workers are deployed.

The large number of detailed job descriptions which exist in mass production firms underlines the narrow range of functions and responsibilities assigned to people.[1] Several highly specialized managers will typically supervise a greater number of skilled and semi-skilled workers, with each of these groups perform-ing different functions in different departments. Matters relating to quality are not spared in the drive to specialize. The mass production firm will usually include a separate department for quality control and quality assurance. Unfortunately, these departments are frequently just another area of specializa-tion to which top managers delegate the critical responsibility for improvement.

The skills developed by managers depend mainly on the experience gained in their respective fields. Many have served in only one department during their career and this background lends a certain bias to their views of the firm's operation.[2] Similar comments apply to those at lower levels in the organization. They carry out fairly specialized assignments and their attention focuses on the immediate requirements of their job and department. In brief, the system creates a workforce of specialists who are more concerned with their own agenda rather than with the needs of customers, fellow employees or the overall firm (Stahl and Bounds, 1991, p. 11). The result is likely to be an excessive degree of competition and rivalry between departments, frustrating attempts to share information or collaborate on programmes for improvement.

The firm's incentive systems and criteria for judging the performance of people reinforce this pattern of specialization. Managers and their subordinates are all under pressure to meet specific goals for their department, work shift or some other organizational group. Under such conditions, people will gain little by sharing information or ideas with others. Each departmental entity comes to resemble an 'organizational silo' which resists the cross-departmental flows of information and ideas that could increase customer value. Not surprisingly, a paradoxical situation can arise where the achievement of departmental goals actually contributes to overall customer dissatisfaction or a decline in the firm's market share (see Box 3.1).

Similar priorities apply with regard to the collection, processing and use of production-related data. Mass production firms generally have sophisticated systems for this purpose. Much of the information is collected by workers at assembly lines, loading docks or inventory warehouses. After analysis and

**Box 3.1   Is management by objective an effective approach?**

The premise for management by objective (MBO) is simple: creative managers and workers are expected to perform more effectively if confronted with an appropriate mixture of incentives and deterrents. The drawback is that in firms where employees and machinery are highly specialized, workers strongly identify with their own speciality while ignoring the interests of other departments or the firm as a whole. In such circumstances the achievement of most goals or objectives could actually lead to a deterioration in overall performance. For instance, the sales department may meet its higher target only to find out that the production can not be delivered. Similarly, a production department may increase output but release more defective items in order to meet its new quota. Purchasing departments can slash costs by pitting one supplier against others or by accepting the lowest bid from an unknown vendor. A danger is that materials are of questionable quality or are not delivered on time. Despite results such as these, employees and departments that meet or exceed their objectives will be lauded, even though the firm and its customers are not well served.

processing by specialists, it is transferred through various functional levels of the firm to the higher echelons of management. Eventually, the data is used to develop production plans, determine directives and set standards which then filter back down through the hierarchy to the production site. This circular flow of information through the firm reflects a clear distinction between the tasks of thinking and doing or the 'brains' and the 'hands' of the organization (Florida and Kenney, 1990, p.12). Very simply stated, managers are paid to think and plan while workers are paid to perform the tasks necessary to carry out the plans.

Well-run systems of this type can efficiently handle quantitative data but are less effective when the information is informal in character. The mass producer's limited ability to process the latter sort of information can be attributed to several factors:

- Decision makers are often ill-equipped to evaluate informal information.

- Long periods of time may elapse before data is translated into an action or decision. Such delays are not practical in the case of informal data since its usefulness decays rapidly.

- The principles which govern operation of traditional information systems tend to discourage the collection and sharing of informal data.

- Informal data does not travel well within mass production firms.

Failures such as these mean that many opportunities to introduce improvements in products or processes are squandered. Below, we look at each of these characteristics in more detail.

Top managers are primarily interested in measurable results that refer to the firm as a whole. Their subordinates are expected to resolve problems on the shop floor and to deal with informal types of information relating to production sites. Because few executives have any experience working on the production line, informal information may have little meaning for them. Their difficulties are compounded by the fact that the workers having the greatest knowledge in this area are excluded from the decision-making process. The result is that much valuable information never reaches the upper echelons of management. When such information does land on managers' desks, it is usually at a time of crisis — for example, when a shipment of defective items is supplied to a customer or an expensive piece of machinery breaks down. The crisis will be quickly resolved but little thought may be given to the underlying reasons for its occurrence.

The effectiveness of informal information is further impaired by the time lag between collection at the work site and corrective action by managers. Whether information concerns defects, customers' orders or design and engineering problems, it must first travel up through the organizational hierarchy to a remote decision-making centre. Even if the information is promptly transferred, top managers may make no decisions until they begin the next round of planning. Valuable time for making corrections and improvements is lost in either case. New office technologies can speed the physical transmission of data but the fundamental problem is not resolved. Simply stated, the value of site-specific information decays rapidly as it moves up and down the organizational ladder.

Yet another problem is that many information systems implicitly assign a low priority to informal sources. A tacit assumption is that direct labour has little to offer besides the performance of its defined job. The implication is not lost on workers who recognize that they are not paid to think or improve the process. Some simply assume a role which confirms common managerial stereotypes about careless or shoddy methods. Many will be aware that they incur risks when they make suggestions or identify problems on the shop floor. Fear of an argument or even personal blame often prevents the worker from speaking up, even if there is strong evidence to support his suggestion (see Walton, 1989, p.71). Other reasons for reticence include: fear of the consequences if a proposal is tried and fails, concern about job security and the prospects for promotion, or the tacit assumption that management is already aware of the problem.[3]

Finally, informal data does not travel well within traditional information systems. Quantitative measures such as counts of defects, volume of rework or product throughput can be easily transferred from the work site to the manager's desk but such data does not present a complete picture. Informal information referring to a particular situation or work site can be difficult to communicate to persons who are far removed from the shop floor. Successful information transfers between workers and line supervisors or foremen are possible but they rarely extend to higher levels (see Box 3.2). If top managers receive such data at all, it is second-hand and largely out of context.

As competition has intensified, managers have recognized some of these weaknesses and sought to address them. Their responses are sometimes very ambitious. Many large firms have eliminated whole layers of middle management, undertaking drastic forms of restructuring or withdrawing from certain product markets. In such instances the desire to improve methods of gathering and interpreting information are part of a much larger agenda.[4] Some managers opt for more pragmatic solutions, frequently choosing to focus on improvements in their information systems. Popular examples include: efforts to capture and utilize informal information more effectively, programmes to eliminate functional barriers that slow the firm's rate of improvement or attempts to encourage the flow of information and ideas across departmental boundaries. In brief, improvements in the information system may be part of a larger set of remedial actions or they may represent a primary goal in more modest attempts to boost competitiveness. Below we consider three of the latter options in order to learn a bit more about the mass producer's ability to modify its information-gathering process. They include:

- the creation of quality control circles;

---

**Box 3.2    Ad hoc systems to handle informal information**

Despite a lack of encouragement, a few workers informally pursue their ideas for improvements without managerial support or interference. A drawback is that these activities are not built into the system and are usually unrecorded. When a key employee leaves the firm, his replacement may lack the experience, contacts or personality to continue the operation. Ad hoc methods of information exchange can also be undercut by a new manager who discovers unauthorized improvements and decides to return operations to their original state. Decision makers in mass production firms may obtain informal information through means such as these but the system's success depends on the strength of personality and the dogged persistence of individual workers, rather than any formal and open channel of shared information. Ultimately, these obstacles to information flows and ideas are one of the barriers that rob people of the pride of workmanship (Deming, 1986).

- efforts to develop informal channels of communication within the firm; and

- programmes to encourage the flow of information from workers to managers.

Inspired by the success of Japanese firms, manufacturers in other industrialized countries have embraced the idea of the 'quality control circle' (QCC). These groups are composed of representatives from different departments who are expected to share their ideas and discuss methods to improve quality and efficiency. Some quality circles have achieved good results, though others have not lived up to expectations (Bradley and Hill, 1987). Many reasons have been suggested for the poor performance of these groups (see Hill, 1991).

One recurrent explanation for these failures is that the organizational structure of mass production firms limits the QCC's effectiveness. Firms that perfected this method were already organized along lines that assigned a high priority to collaborative work on improvements. Those geared to produce according to methods of mass production rarely provide the types of incentives that would bolster the work of quality groups.[5] As a result, participation in a QCC is an assignment in addition to usual job responsibilities. The role played by middle managers can be particularly awkward. They are charged with overseeing these groups but have no authority to implement any changes the QCC proposes. The effectiveness of quality circles can be further diminished because recommendations cut across departmental boundaries or exceed the group's narrowly-defined mandate. Finally, the active interest of top managers tends to be short-lived, declining rapidly after an initial burst of enthusiasm (Hill, 1991, p. 549).

A different approach is to establish more direct communication between managers and workers. Often, a method known as 'management by walking around' is used for this purpose. Managers seek to learn more about the current situation by leaving their offices and talking with experienced workers on the shop floor. Based on these discussions, they may make suggestions or initiate changes in manufacturing processes. The tactic can backfire if it reveals just how disconnected from day-to-day operations managers really are. Another weakness is that anecdotal evidence is no substitute for a thorough knowledge of on-site operations and efficient systems to turn shop-floor information into genuine improvements. The end result may be little more than sporadic communication between management and workers.

Programmes to encourage the flow of information from workers to managers take many forms. Examples include: regular or periodic meetings of workers and managers, 'open door' policies where workers are invited to discuss issues of quality and improvement with managers, seminars on improvement issues, programmes to encourage employee suggestions and so on.[6] None of these methods are likely to succeed unless managerial attitudes and organizational structures are fundamentally altered. The outcome can be particularly disappointing for companies where labour–management relations are poor. Suspicious workers regard these initiatives as another way to reduce their numbers or to wring more work out of existing staff. The paradoxical result could be that programmes for improvement actually lead to a decrease in productivity.

In summary, the search for internal improvements is often thwarted by the separation of functions and high degree of specialization which is so common in many mass production firms. These characteristics inhibit the flow of production information and ideas that are critical for continuous improvement. Despite such handicaps, many top managers prefer to address their informational problems by methods which leave the basic structure of their organization intact. The following section looks at the opposite end of our stylistic spectrum and asks whether the mass producer can borrow any methods and tools from the continuous improvement firm.

## ORGANIZATIONAL BARRIERS AND MISCONCEPTIONS

Continuous improvement is distinguished from other attempts to increase productivity and bolster competitiveness by its emphasis on daily, incremental forms of improvement. The purpose of all these efforts is to enhance customer value, a concept which refers not only to price but attributes of product quality, product design, serviceability, durability and other ways of boosting customer satisfaction. The critical link between information and customer satisfaction requires that managers create and nurture the work of groups whose intellectual capabilities produce customer value.[7]

Like any other manufacturer, the overriding goals of a CIF are obvious ones such as increased market share or profitability. However, the way in which the firm pursues these goals in its day-to-day operations is sometimes obscure, at least to the outside observer. The sorts of improvements which typify daily operations are usually minuscule and often undocumented. Outsiders tend to overlook this dogged process of minor improvements and are unlikely to comprehend the system that nourishes it.

Not surprisingly, a firm that embarks on a programme of continuous improvement may underestimate the magnitude of its task. Many managers erroneously assume that the transformation can be accomplished by simply purchasing a 'package' of statistical tools and other production techniques and then installing them like a piece of capital equipment. This misjudgement is compounded by a tendency to focus on some dramatic result rather than the process of improvement itself. One example is the development of just-in-time (JIT) methods of inventory control. Many observers hailed this achievement as a 'revolutionary breakthrough', though in reality it was the outcome of 30 years of evolutionary, incremental improvements (see Nayak and Ketteringham, 1986). The same applies to other aspects of continuous improvement such as SMED, statistical process control, quality control circles and Japanese techniques like kanban and pokayoke.[8]

Firms may be poorly prepared to make the transition to continuous improvement but nevertheless begin with an evangelical zeal. Employees are exhorted to become part of the campaign for 'total quality', 'zero defects', 'world-class manufacturing', JIT or some other label. Consultants, quality circles and programmes of 'employee involvement' are conspicuous during this early phase. Productivity and product quality will usually show some improvement, but all too often these gains are short-lived. When the initial momentum dissipates, managers realize that they have invested considerable amounts of money and time for only modest returns in productivity and quality. One result is that programmes for 'quality and improvement' lose credibility among both managers and workers.

Why do these tools sometimes lose their potency when transferred to new practitioners of continuous improvement? First, a great deal of the know-how embodied in techniques such as JIT, quality control circles or SPC is company-specific. Such methods have been adapted and refined through years of experience and are now deeply embedded in the culture of the CIF (see Box 3.3). Newcomers can not hope to assimilate these routines into their company quickly. Nor can they expect that the original methods will be ideally suited to their factory's environment; further adaptations will almost certainly be necessary. These tasks become even more difficult if the firm's existing organizational structure is relatively inflexible.

Second, the newcomer is at a disadvantage owing to the rapid pace of change. Long-time practitioners of continuous improvement are constantly refining existing techniques and developing new ones. They have accumulated years of experience and created a work environment that encourages change. Meanwhile, the new adherent struggles to master methods which may only remain state-of-the-art for a brief period. Without constant information exchange and a system to coordinate the search for improvements, the new convert may never overtake its better-organized rivals.

The barriers encountered by the newcomer can be illustrated by considering the hypothetical case of a typical mass production firm that competes against a CIF of similar size. Over time, the latter firm has achieved a position of superiority which can be explained in terms of product quality, price advantages, service practices or other product characteristics. Suppose that managers of the mass production firm conclude that their rival's success is largely due to

**Box 3.3 Successes and failures in improvement programmes**

Around three-quarters of all manufacturing and service companies in the United States and the United Kingdom claim to operate programmes dealing with continuous improvement, quality control or related goals. Yet recent surveys indicate that only a minority are satisfied with the results. In the United States, for example, a survey of 500 manufacturing and service companies found that only a third believed the programmes have a 'significant impact' on their competitiveness. Another survey of 100 firms in the United Kingdom revealed that only a fifth regarded their programmes as having 'tangible results'.

Why is the number of satisfied companies not higher? First, many managers expect the programmes to be a swift and sure way to reverse their firm's declining fortunes. However, years may be required to assimilate these routines and to modify and adapt them to every part of the firm's operation. Nor will improvements in quality offset the effects of an inferior product or an industry-wide decline in demand. Second, companies outside Japan lack experience in implementing such programmes. Evidence to support both these points can be found in the following chart. Many of the successful Japanese companies have three to four decades of experience in this field. Firms in the United States have considerably less experience. All, however, take a long-term view of quality and improvement.

*Number of years' experience with total-quality management*

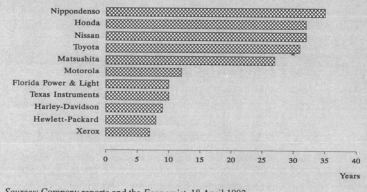

*Sources*: Company reports and the *Economist*, 18 April 1992.

its skilful use of statistical tools. They hope to strengthen their own firm's position by introducing a rigorous programme of SPC. Consultants are engaged to assist in this undertaking, several managers and line workers are trained in data analysis and data collection, and every assembly line soon bristles with control charts. Over the next few years, the mass producer's efforts yield results as defects, rework and customer complaints are reduced. But surprisingly, the gap between the two firms does not diminish. The CIF introduces improvements of its own which preserve its position of leadership. This outcome prompts the mass producer to re-evaluate its competitor's operations. An investigation reveals that most of the statistical charts and related tools which were so much in evidence in the CIF's plants only a few years before have disappeared.

How can this apparent reversal of production methods be explained? The CIF did not abandon its original philosophy once the manufacturing system was brought under statistical control. Instead, it progressed to a new, more sophisticated level of operation which no longer requires extensive use of SPC. Special causes of variation were first eliminated and steps taken to ensure that they did not recur. Following this phase, common causes of variation were attacked. Process variation was gradually reduced so that parts could be designed to more precise specifications and tolerances. Manufacturing processes and products were regularly reconfigured in order to 'design variation out of the system'. Eventually, the need to monitor each process through statistical means became unnecessary.

The danger which this example illustrates is that the mass production firm may become 'stuck' in the early stages of SPC.[9] Meanwhile, the CIF moves on to a more sophisticated level of application. The distinction between the two firms is partly due to their disparate approaches to the problem of common-cause variation. The CIF is prepared to adapt, alter or refine any aspect of its production system — from design to delivery. Managers, line workers, and technicians collaborate to obtain *all* the production-related information needed to guide the firm in its search for improvement. The mass producer, though a voracious consumer of the more conventional forms of quantitative data, makes little use of informal types of information. Nor are its managers willing to consider the more radical forms of change in organizational and managerial structure which are necessary to remove this bottleneck.

It is not surprising that the mass producer is disappointed with the results of this experiment. SPC is a set of statistical tools which can be used to bring manufacturing processes under control (that is, to eliminate special causes of variation) and afterwards to reduce variation due to common causes. Once these goals have been achieved, the tools should be dismantled and moved elsewhere. Lacking the proper information and unwilling to make the changes needed to secure that data, the mass production firm cannot rid itself of common-cause variation. Statistical charts and related devices become a permanent feature of its operation. In that capacity they are the graphical counterpart of an inspector, serving merely as insurance against a loss of statistical control.

Some tools of continuous improvement can be quickly integrated into a firm's operation though others require several years for experimentation and adaptation. During that time a large number of changes and modifications will have to be made. The basic role of managers must be altered, as will every aspect of existing production routines and workers' responsibilities. These adjustments will be conditioned by the technologies installed. Meanwhile, the technologies themselves must be tailored to suit the host company's environment. Without adaptation, a CIT may never become an integral part of the firm's production system. It is reasonable to expect that some alterations will be necessary when these techniques are transferred from one company to another.

In summary, mass production firms rarely capitalize upon the on-site information which is essential if newly-acquired CITs are to be efficiently assimilated. Nor are these firms willing to contemplate the changes in managerial attitudes and organizational structure that are necessary to compile and use this sort of information. No such restrictions apply to the CIF. Its organization and methods of operation are designed to make optimal use of on-site information to promote improvements in product quality, process efficiency and flexibility (see Bós, 1991, pp. 25–33). With these advantages, the CIF is in a better position to integrate new methods into its production system quickly and then go on to refine and adapt these methods to suit its specific needs.

The CIF's superior use of information can be attributed to several factors:

- Managers and workers in the CIF are better prepared to deal with a diverse set of problems simultaneously. They have a broader range of work experience and encounter few barriers which discourage information flows and collaboration between groups. Horizontal coordination of operating units in the CIF is founded on shared information rather than skill specialization.

- There is a collective approach to problem-solving which ensures a company-wide perspective. This orientation is essential if new technologies are to be adapted and refined to suit a company's specific needs.

- Production-line workers are given greater autonomy and decision-making authority than in traditional firms. There is no sharp demarcation in the CIF between 'thinking' and 'doing' activities.

A firm's conversion to continuous improvement will inevitably create difficulties during the break-in period. Problems involving matters ranging from cost to design, quality and production scheduling spill across departmental boundaries and fields of responsibility. Furthermore, these issues must be addressed simultaneously if the new techniques are to be efficiently mastered and assimilated.[10]  All this requires a company-wide effort which can not succeed without coordination and collaboration.  A mass production firm with a highly specialized workforce and an elaborate division of responsibilities will find it difficult to make these adjustments in a timely manner.

Employees in a CIF tend to be better equipped to handle a diverse range of problems at the same time.  While tasks are specialized, workers are generalized (Cole, 1992).  For example, the number of job descriptions and work-related classifications found in the CIF are far fewer than for the typical mass producer.  The CIF takes every opportunity to ensure that its people gain experience in several departments and tasks.  Job rotation and group work provide managers, technical personnel and shop-floor employees with a broader view of the organic workings of the enterprise.  Once the CIF has created an experienced workforce, it maximizes the benefits by eliminating any existing barriers between areas of staff responsibility.  One way of doing this is to encourage the workers' participation in groups such as QCCs.  Another is to remove any disincentives to collaborate across functions.[11]  Sometimes, physical barriers — for example, walls and partitions between staff areas — will be removed as well.  Through these means, employees gain a broad understanding of each other's role and are better able to cooperate in the creation of customer value.

A collective approach to decision-making follows naturally from arrangements such as these.[12]  Many CIFs hold informal meetings at the beginning of the day to discuss major issues.  Cross-functional groups which include managers, technicians and hourly workers from different departments are also common.  Formal groups are expected to address different problems on a regular basis while informal ones may be convened to deal with problems as they arise.  Unlike their equivalents in traditional firms, these groups have the authority to enact changes after they have studied a problem and agreed upon a solution.  Meetings provide opportunities to share critical, on-site information with colleagues who have different responsibilities and functions.  Each team has the same set of very precise goals: to find ways to eliminate defects or to introduce improvements which will be of benefit to the 'customer'.  Importantly, their deliberations take into account both external and internal customers.  The external customer is the purchaser of the finished product and the final arbiter of quality while the internal customers are those employees who will subsequently work on a partly finished product as it moves through the manufacturing system.  The satisfaction of each customer, whether internal or external, is the concern of every group.  The outcome of all this group activity is a constant flow of small improvements.  Few, if any, of these changes will be documented or written down in any formal way.  Nevertheless, they are widely discussed by all involved and quickly become part of standard practice (see

Box 3.4). Without such effective methods for the exchange of information and opinion, cooperation across functions and departments deteriorates and the effectiveness of CIT is jeopardized.

A third method to ensure effective use of informal information is to grant workers the authority to make changes at the work site. Because these employees have the deepest understanding of a particular manufacturing process, they are in the best position to make decisions of this sort. Whether the modifications emerge from group discussions or are made on an individual basis is immaterial; the important point is that workers are expected to improve production processes.[13] This limited delegation of authority does not mean that managers are freed from leadership responsibilities. It does imply that in the area of improvement workers need not always be followers.

The expectation is that workers who can exercise authority at the work site will have more pride in their jobs and take results seriously. Such an environment does not depend on workshops, lectures, sensitivity-training sessions, employee retreats or slogans. Nor is it contingent on the rhetoric of consultants who preach 'employee involvement', 'job enrichment' or 'quality-of-life programmes'. To be successful, managers must create a system which maximizes the experience, collaborative instincts and information of workers; and then reconfirm their commitment to this system on a daily basis.

---

**Box 3.4   Documenting production-line changes in the CIF**

The CIF depends on a free flow of information between different groups and job functions. A properly working system of information exchange means there is less need to commit precise instructions to writing. Moreover, change is continuous and many adaptations have only a short life span. A convenient way to represent the latest round of improvements may be a temporary visual aid (for example, a blackboard or bulletin board) located in the work area where everyone sees it. Recent changes would then be obvious to anyone from outside the immediate work area. Such visual aids can also be a powerful stimulant to further discussion on improvements. The same practice would be risky in conventional firms where managers plan all production-line modifications and workers implement these plans. Written documentation will usually be required to avoid ambiguities and misinterpretations. This top-down form of management means that a great deal of the production-line information possessed by workers is lost, ignored or decays rapidly. Workers quickly learn to anticipate the next round of instructions rather than to think in terms of improvement. In such firms there are few visual aids referring to improvement activities although there could be an abundance of posters and slogans exhorting workers to strive for greater quality and performance.

## CONCEPTS OF TIME AND EFFICIENCY

Production efficiency can be defined as the goal of maximizing output with the minimum amount of inputs. Time has an important role to play in this equation. A factory's costs will rise when the period of operating time in any given week or month is lengthened. It follows that costs per unit of output will decline if the production target can be met in a shorter period of time. In other words, a firm that can manufacture the same number of units as its rival more quickly, and do that without additional inputs or equipment, will be more efficient.

Ideas such as these might appear to be so fundamental that they allow no alternative interpretations. Yet the CIF and mass producer have quite different views of time and efficiency. In the mass production firm the two concepts are merged in the search for 'economies of time' (see Best, 1990, pp. 147–56; and Chandler, 1977). In order to achieve greater economies of time, the firm seeks to maximize the number of items produced in a given period of time. Managers therefore look for ways to speed the movement of materials and semi-finished products through the plant. Greater efficiency and lower production costs of standardized products are the result.

The mass producer bases its search for economies of time on two fundamental guidelines. One, known as 'the principle of flow', was developed by engineers in the early twentieth century. This innovation led to the redesign of the factory floor, so the 'flowline' of machines would conform with the sequence of machining operations. The step was a great improvement over earlier methods which required that batches of material or product be moved from one specialized department to the next. Engineers subsequently went on to devise more sophisticated flowlines for products which were assembled from a series of components. All these efforts came together in the automobile industry where the principle of flow was successfully employed to manufacture a product requiring a large number of complex components.

Methods of scientific management were developed at about the same time as the principle of flow and served as a second guideline in the search for economies of time. Closely associated with the research of Frederick Taylor, scientific management required that production-line activities be carefully synchronized with the flow of production.[14] High rates of throughput meant that workers must perform routine, repetitive tasks with machinery that was running at full capacity.

With better planning of a factory's machine layout and careful organization of workers' routines, managers were able to achieve large increases in throughput at much lower unit costs.[15] Work activities were constantly redefined in ways that distinguished between managers' planning responsibilities and workers' manual tasks. This version of mass production was soon transferred from the United States to other industrialized countries, becoming the dominant organizational model for all large manufacturers by the mid-twentieth century. Because the model focuses on the productive time needed to transform material into products, measures such as productivity per labour hour or machine output per hour are the accepted yardsticks for measuring operational efficiency.

Interpretations of efficiency and time have evolved along quite different lines in the CIF. Forerunners of the modern CIF recognized that the ability to reduce manufacturing overheads would be a key to competitive success. These overheads include expenditures relating to inventory, materials handling, inspection, warehouses, resource planning, changeover and quality control. For the typical mass producer, they can amount to 200 per cent or more of direct labour costs.[16] By reducing process variation and cutting back on product lines, the early CIFs were able to lower manufacturing overheads substantially. This gave them a cost advantage over rival firms using methods of mass production (Abegglen and Stalk, 1985).

The CIFs made aggressive use of their cost advantage but could still supply only a limited number of products or models. The problem, which they shared with mass manufacturers, was that overheads rose exponentially whenever the number of product lines was increased. Burgeoning overheads resulted from the larger number of parts that were required, the diverse range of problems encountered and greater complexity of the manufacturing processes. After many years of experimentation, this problem was resolved by development of the JIT production system in the 1970s. Japanese firms found they were able to manufacture different products on the same production line without driving up overhead costs. Their success meant that the mass producer was now confronted by a flexible, low-cost rival who could compete across a wide range of product lines.

The CIF's improved ability to control overhead costs led to new views of efficiency which recognized that not all a firm's activities and associated costs are a direct result of the manufacturing processes. Only a portion of total production time is actually used to turn inputs and materials into finished products. Alongside these value-adding activities are various auxiliary functions which contribute to costs but add no value to the finished product. Workers, for example, devote some portion of their time to inventories and other 'non-productive' assignments involving inspections, reworking components and products or moving, storing and counting items and products.

All manufacturers, both CIFs and mass producers, are concerned with the amount of productive time required to convert materials into finished products. They express the costs of productive time in terms of operational efficiency, a concept which refers to the direct involvement of people and machines in the value-adding activities of the firm. The CIF carries this analysis further; it will also monitor the costs of auxiliary functions. Managers then construct measures of efficiency which take into account the costs of auxiliary (indirect) activities as well as direct involvement in the production process. One example of such a measure is the idea of 'process-throughput efficiency' which is defined as the amount of time materials and components are actually being worked on divided by the total amount of time these inputs spend in the production system.

Estimates of process-throughput efficiency provide the CIF with an indication of how much indirect activities contribute to manufacturing overheads and total costs. However, they give no information about the way inventories affect overheads. To take this element into account, other measures focus attention on work-in-process (WIP), which is defined as the value of production inventory less the value of finished products ready for shipping. A large inventory of WIP requires employees to spend a considerable portion of their time counting, handling, storing, processing and expediting shipment. These indirect activities are necessary because inventories are high. However, they are also expensive and add nothing to the value of the product. Savings are possible by reducing the size of WIP inventories for a given level of output or by accelerating the movement of WIP through the factory. This 'leanness in production' can be measured by stock-turnover figures, which are defined as the value of raw materials, work-in-process, and finished products, all expressed as a percentage of total sales.[17]

These different interpretations of time and efficiency naturally lead to divergent methods and strategies of production. The mass production firm's emphasis on operational efficiency leads managers to explain a factory's poor competitive performance in terms of labour costs and levels of direct labour productivity. It follows that cost-cutting efforts will usually focus on ways to increase labour and capital productivity rather than reducing the extent of indirect activities (Johnson and Kaplan, 1987, Chapter 8). The difficulty with such an approach is that the search for costs savings is confined to productive time — that is, the small percentage of time in which value-adding production activities occur. Much greater amounts of time may be absorbed by indirect activities which the exercise ignores. This limitation is underlined by recent estimates of process-throughput efficiency. For plants in the United States and the United Kingdom, value-adding operations account for as little as 1 to 2.5 per cent of the time that materials and other inputs spend in the plant. In other words, these materials are untouched for as much as 99 per cent of the time. The efficiency of process-throughput rarely exceeds 20 per cent of total time, even in high-volume assembly operations (New, 1988, p. 1).

If a firm's efforts to bolster its competitive position are confined to improvements in operational efficiency, the net effect can sometimes be negative. Additional pressure on direct workers may be of no benefit if it drives up the rate of defects and amount of rework. Diminished worker morale and falling rates of productivity are other possible consequences. Wage cuts, a reduction in the number of production-line workers, a cutback in the volume of production or elimination of certain product lines are other options. Any of these steps could be necessary, but it is also possible that they could be avoided if the firm sought productivity improvements by eliminating some of its indirect or auxiliary activities.

The CIF tends to take a system-wide approach in its search for ways to improve operation and process efficiency. Managers and workers collaborate effectively to gather and utilize information which can reduce process variation, waste and overhead costs. These go hand in hand with increased product quality and deliverability. The fact that costs can decline while quality increases is a direct challenge to the conventional wisdom embodied in the mass production organization.

## NOTES

1. The CIF will have a much smaller number of job descriptions. In some cases, the worker has considerable freedom to write his own job description.
2. Managers with long experience in a single field may rely heavily on financial and accounting tools that understate or overlook altogether the role of quality and improvement. Furthermore, where there are rigidly defined departments the top manager who has risen through the ranks in one function can be the object of suspicion on the part of those in different specialities.
3. In many instances supervisors and managers belatedly recognize a glaring problem and are then perplexed because workers on the floor had not mentioned it to them earlier. Often, the workers had simply assumed that managers were already aware of the situation. Better channels of communication would have ensured that this information was immediately available.
4. The current wave of downsizing in large corporations is frequently — but inaccurately — linked to programmes of 'quality improvement'. Understandably, many workers assume that their jobs are being threatened when their firm embarks on any improvement programme. These fears can render all discussion of teamwork, empowerment, investment in people and the like as so many hollow phrases (Kuttner, 1993, p.12). In the CIF it is more likely that programmes to increase productivity are accompanied by worker retraining so that people can perform new tasks.
5. These groups have various titles such as quality control circles, quality assurance teams, quality deployment teams, zero defect groups and so on.
6. Many mass production firms have experimented with suggestion systems but the results are frequently disappointing. One reason is that management accepts few of the suggestions, or that it implements some but fails to recognize the originator. The net effect of such programmes on employee moral can also be negative. Financial incentives may lead to a flurry of suggestions, but in firms where programmes of continuous improvement are not deeply entrenched, the suggestions end if incentives are discontinued.
7. In the CIF, it is intellectual capital, not equipment, that is managed (Jaikumar, 1986, p. 75).
8. Pokayoke refers to a simple system of 'mistake-proofing' which depends on simple devices or routines that help to prevent human error. Kanban refers to a system of visual inventory controls that form an integral part of many JIT systems. In its simplest form, individual items or lots in inventory are tagged with a kanban card that allows the producer to trace the flows of material in production. Cards are removed as inventory items enter the process which then serve as a visual signal for reordering. These practices are discussed in more detail in Chapter 4.

9. This applies to many improvement programmes such as quality control circles, various forms of JIT and other methods.

10. Once continuous improvement is fully incorporated into an enterprise, incremental improvements come at little or no expense to other productive activities. For example, where operators on the line serve as their own inspectors and communicate with the next person in the process, modest adjustments can be made that both expedite flow and reduce defects. However, during the transition to continuous improvement, there can be considerable costs. The costs that are most difficult to measure are the inefficiencies that occur because of resistance to change on the part of some managers and section heads.

11. For example, annual ratings systems discourage effective teamwork. The main reason is that work spent on a team comes at the expense of performance for which an individual or department is measured and evaluated. Managers may actually tell subordinates not to spend much time or effort on group work because of duties in their own department.

12. Studies of managerial practices in Japan and the United States reveal two observable differences in the decision-making process. First, there is much more communication at lower levels of management in Japanese companies which then percolates upward. Second, while both groups of managers rated the quality of their own decision-making skills as about the same, Japanese managers believe their ability to implement these decisions is superior (Pascale, 1992, p. 124).

13. If workers have some decision-making authority and a strong commitment to the firm's goals, they will support a suggestion system. For example, in the typical CIF employees make many suggestions and a relatively high percentage are implemented. Managers will also be careful to follow up on the suggestions they implement. The benefits of the improvement, in terms of savings of time, money and effort, are also displayed along with the name of the person making the suggestion.

14. Taylor was an organizational innovator in the late nineteenth century who studied production activity on the shop floor in order to increase throughput. His name is most closely associated with 'time and motion' studies in which he sought to match the movements of workers with the flow of material through a factory. Such movements were to be planned down to the smallest detail. Taylor also established the idea of incentive pay as a cornerstone of scientific management, arguing that workers should be paid differential rates according to whether they met or exceeded 'standard' amounts of output. Wages became a function of job evaluation and job classification rather than workers' skills. Union activity became ever more involved with job classifications and seniority rights (Best, 1990, Chapter 2).

15. Ford Motor Company was one of the first manufacturers to demonstrate effective application of scientific management and the principle of the flow. In 1909 luxury cars were selling in the United States for over $4,000, but the price of a Model T was only $950 and was cut to $360 by 1916. Meanwhile, sales grew from 12,000 to 577,000 cars (Hounshell, quoted in Best, 1990, p. 71).

16. 'Direct labour' is labour that adds value directly to the final product (for example, workers performing assembly on the line). 'Indirect labour' involves the support activities such as warehousing or accounting. Those involved in support activities do not work directly with the product.

17. A related measure of process efficiency is the WIP turn, which is analogous to the stock–turnover ratio first used by mass retailers. The more times that a given amount of WIP is turned over in some time period (usually a year), or the more times that a given amount of WIP is converted into finished goods, the higher the process efficiency of the firm. A rule of thumb is that every time the WIP turn doubles, labour productivity increases by around 38 per cent (see Best, 1990, p.148).

# 4. Working Tools of Continuous Improvement

CIFs have a wide range of technologies or techniques from which to choose. Several of these are associated mainly with the goal of making products of a higher quality. They can indeed be used for this purpose but when employed in a programme of continuous improvement the objectives are broader. Cost reduction, productivity gains and greater organizational efficiency are the primary goals. Some of the more powerful and better-known techniques are examined in Chapter 4, while the supporting statistical tools are described in Chapter 5.

Because continuous improvement is a dynamic process which offers a large number of different technologies, the selection process is more an art than a science. Firms that cling to the same techniques will lose out to their more flexible and aggressive rivals. In some instances the technologies originally employed will have already enriched the improvement programme and should be replaced with more sophisticated techniques. In other cases a technique is refined and altered so drastically that it bears little resemblance to the original procedure.

Many technologies are available to the CIF and only a sampling can be described here. Not all options are equally suitable for any firm and those presented are meant to give some idea of the range of choices available. The discussion begins by reviewing some of the simpler alternatives and then goes on to examine several of the technologies which might be used by firms that have several years of experience with continuous improvement.

## THE PDCA CYCLE

The plan-do-check-act (PDCA) cycle is one of the most powerful, yet simple, forms of continuous improvement.[1] It depends on scientific methods of investigation and can be used to improve both manufacturing processes and products. Companies that are experienced in the application of CITs may no longer make explicit use of this tool, although the procedures they employ to organize the programme of continuous improvement owe much to their earlier mastery of the technique.

The four stages of the PDCA cycle can be described as follows:

- **Planning**. Managers, technical personnel and workers single out a particular manufacturing process or part of the production system with the purpose of identifying those operations that have the greatest potential for improvement. Once this is done, the team agrees on the best means for monitoring and studying each of these steps. Opinions and suggestions are sought from all team members. Finally, a plan is devised which spells out the actions to be taken and the methods of analysis that will be used.

- **Doing/implementation**. The plan is executed. The team will first apply the plan on a small scale if that is possible. Results are carefully monitored and all deviations from the plan should be recorded. Data is collected using some of the tools described in Chapter 5.

- **Checking and verification**. Results are evaluated and compared to the original goals. The group discusses what has been learned from the experiment and determines the potential for improvement.

- **Action**. If the experiment demonstrates that certain steps improve efficiency or quality, these are standardized and become part of day-to-day procedures. The entire cycle is then repeated, meaning that each new set of standards or procedures may apply for only a brief period of time.

## THE SEVEN WASTES

Elimination of wasteful shop-floor practices is one of the first targets of the CIF. For this purpose, waste is defined as any operation which adds no value to the product but increases costs.[2] Evidence is easy to compile, yet a surprisingly large proportion of all shop-floor activities generate no added value. It is not unusual that materials and parts are worked on only two or three per cent of the time they spend in the plant. During other periods they are stored, moved from one location to another, packed, unpacked or inspected — all activities that add no value to the finished product.

Other common forms of waste occur when unneeded or defective parts are produced or when machines are idle during set-up or because of breakdowns.

The end result is that a substantial proportion of the total operating time of a typical factory is absorbed by activities which add no value to the finished product but that have a significant impact on costs. Seven of the most common areas of waste in a plant have been identified by Suzaki (1987, pp. 7–24) and are summarized below.

- **Overproduction** is one of the most costly and common sources of waste. Yet it is often ignored until market demand slumps. At that point the costs of overproduction multiply owing to a build-up of unsold goods in inventory and the additional expenses incurred for handling, storage, interest charges and other activities which add no value.

- **The time workers spend waiting** for materials to be delivered, for a machine to be repaired, or for paperwork to be completed is an obvious form of waste. A less visible form of waste occurs in mass production and other inspection-dependent factories where workers are expected to watch machines and take corrective action when a problem arises. The CIF combats these problems by streamlining the flow of materials and paperwork. Sometimes, machines can be fitted with simple devices which automatically shut down production or provide an audible warning when a malfunction occurs. Operators can then divide their attention between the task of attending a machine and other jobs (for example, maintenance). Frequently they can tend to more than one machine at a time.

- **Transportation** is a major source of inefficiency if materials are moved around a factory several times before reaching a point where value is added. Staff must plan these movements, arrange for materials to be stored, picked up, delivered and collected from the production line. Especially long production lines may require temporary storage stations which greatly complicate the tracking of parts and materials. The CIF will cut transport waste by improving the layout of the plant, by meticulous coordination of production processes, more efficient methods of transportation, and better organization of the workplace.

- **Manufacturing processes** are themselves a source of waste. If tools are not properly adjusted or maintained, additional workers are needed to finish, file, paint or complete a product. When materials are not properly prepared for processing, operators must spend more time converting these into products. Managers and workers in the CIF will continually modify or redesign a manufacturing process to reduce the time lost in these ways.

- **Excessive inventories** are more than a temporary problem resulting from swings in demand. They impede the establishment of production priorities and prevent workers from focusing on the tasks at hand. Costly misjudgements can result. For example, because operators are unnecessarily busy and machines are occupied, managers may purchase additional equipment on the erroneous assumption that it is needed. The CIF has a number of tools in its arsenal to combat inventory wastage (see Box 4.1).

- **Unnecessary movement** of workers represents wasted effort which adds to costs. Yet it is common to observe employees in large factories busily searching for their tools, parts or papers. If managers do not recognize these practices as a source of inefficiency, they may demand greater effort or even hire more workers. A much more effective approach is to reduce the need for workers' movements by optimizing the location of tools, parts and machines.

- **Defective products** contribute to waste in several ways. Defects disrupt the flow of throughput and force operators further down the line to wait. It can be very difficult to isolate these problems if the production cycle is long (20 to 30 days). The CIF constantly strives to reduce this cycle which helps to simplify its effort to eliminate defects. Rework also adds to costs, while a decision to scrap defective items means that material

---

**Box 4.1   Combating inventory build-up in a CIF**

Excessive inventories are an unnecessary source of waste. To minimize this problem, the CIF employs a number of methods. First, unneeded materials are excluded from the workplace and production lines are 'balanced' by producing only the items required for the subsequent step in the process. These practices prevent the accumulation of work-in-process and reduce confusion on the production line. Second, orders are closely coordinated with vendors and large lot sizes are not purchased. The CIF forgoes the volume discounts which suppliers offer with large orders, but the savings from reduced inventory waste should more than offset the higher prices charged by suppliers. Third, the CIF aims at manufacturing only small product lots. Set-up times must therefore be reduced and machinery changeovers made more efficient. Assiduous attention to these eventually leads to a just-in-time (JIT) production system.

and effort are wasted.[3] Separating good parts from bad ones is another cost-adding activity which results from defects. The end result is poorer quality and higher costs of the products delivered to the customer.

## THE 5-S MOVEMENT

To eliminate waste, the CIF creates cross-functional teams of managers, workers and technicians. Many of their solutions derive from very simple ideas. The '5-S Movement'[4] is a popular method of organizing the search for waste in factory management which consists of the following steps:

- **Straighten up the work area**. The factory floor in many large plants is cluttered with unnecessary tools, work-in-process, unused machinery, defective products, parts and other items. In a CIF, employees are expected to keep at the work site only that material necessary for performing their jobs. All unnecessary items should be removed.

- **Put all necessary items in order**. Materials and tools should be arranged so they are available when needed. The plant layout is changed so that the optimal arrangement of tools and workers can be achieved (see Figure 4.1). This eliminates wasted motion, reduces the waiting time of employees and minimizes transportation within the plant.

- **Keep the work site clean and tidy**. Organization and housekeeping practices contribute to product quality, worker morale and efficiency. The CIF stresses the links between sloppy plants and defective products, machinery breakdowns and excessive inventories.

- **Follow procedures in the workshop**. Most shop-floor procedures have been determined after a consensus has been reached between managers, technicians and workers. Once these are in place, everyone from the top executive on down, is expected to comply.

*Figure 4.1   Redesigning the plant layout for greater efficiency*

*The two diagrams shown here document the actual changes made in a production line after applying the 5-S procedures described in the text. Machines were tightly regrouped into cells, large piles of components were replaced by small storage bins and the newly-cleared factory floor was neatly marked with colour-coded lines mapping out the flow of materials. Productivity on some lines increased by up to 30 per cent in the working day after these changes were made. The space needed for some processes was cut in half and work-in-process was reduced considerably. The improved layout allowed some jobs to be combined, freeing these workers for deployment elsewhere in the factory.*

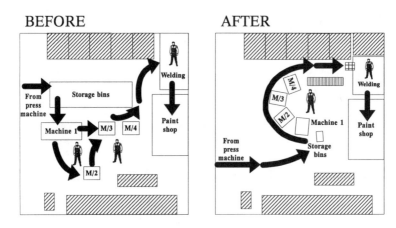

*Source*: UNIDO, based on data reported in the *Financial Times*, 4 January 1994.

## QUALITY DEPLOYMENT

In the 1970s only a few of the world's manufacturers fully incorporated customers' demands into new product designs. However, the situation began to change dramatically in the 1980s. Firms in industrialized countries had learned to make reliable products but they were not good at getting their designs right the first time. New products frequently fell short of customers' expectations and had to be redesigned. Much of the problem was due to lack of information and poor teamwork. Few firms took the trouble to gather data on customers' preferences. Marketing and sales staff had a vague idea of buyers' wishes but were rarely consulted when a new product was planned. Inside the firm, the degree of teamwork was limited. Designers or engineers would put together a new product and the manufacturing department would produce it. This 'over-the-wall' approach where one group passes its work to the next with a minimum of consultation made for high costs and delays.

The consequences of these practices are vividly illustrated by a 1992 survey of firms in the United Kingdom. The results, which are presented in Figure 4.2, show that the bulk of all 'product costs' (that is, all outlays other than operating costs) are determined before production actually begins. The message conveyed by these estimates is clear: the costs of redesign are heavy, not just in terms of customer dissatisfaction and the loss of market share, but also in financial terms.

To avoid such miscues, manufacturers have turned to the idea of 'quality deployment' (QD). The technique is a form of continuous improvement that seeks to identify problems before (not after) they occur. Staff begin by determining customers' requirements and then work backwards to see how they can be met (Fortuna, 1992). Each preference is assigned a priority which

*Figure 4.2   The costs of product development: illustrative trends*

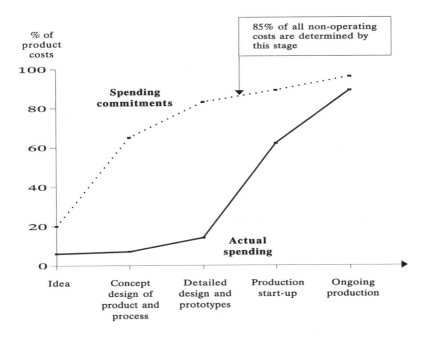

*Source*: Based on information from The Design Council (United Kingdom) cited in the *Financial Times*, 20 April 1993.

is translated into technical specifications at each stage of product development. The need for meticulous planning and analysis means that it may take longer to design a product than with more conventional methods. However, subsequent changes in the design of the product or the manufacturing processes are rare, so the total time required for product development can be reduced by 30 to 50 per cent (Imai, 1986, p.158).

The first step, determination of the customer's needs, can be difficult since buyers are often vague about their preferences. Suppose a vendor of cardboard boxes interviews potential customers who state that they want boxes of precise measurements which are 'light but strong'. The seller's task is to determine exactly what the potential buyer means. What kinds of product will be shipped in these boxes? How much do the products weigh and are they fragile? These are just a few of the questions that the seller asks to determine the needs of the customer.

Once these needs have been defined, the design of the product can be planned. The exact type of cardboard, its thickness, strengths and other critical characteristics must be worked out according to the customer's requirements and the corresponding technical requirements of the manufacturer must be defined. Everything is planned: the precise types of product materials which are needed, the machines and tools to be used, machine adjustments and so on. Specific types of process controls such as SPC, random sampling and maintenance intervals will also be in place before the first box is produced.

All of these steps are carried out by a team drawn from the firm's marketing, engineering and manufacturing operations.[5] Sales and marketing representatives may have a good understanding of the customer but little comprehension of the product's technical aspects. Engineers and designers supply this expertise, although they may have little understanding of what the customer wants. The team stays together throughout the entire design process. In this way they gain a critical stake in the delivery of a product that the customer wants.

As firms gain experience in QD, their ambitions grow. They will want to know what characteristics consumers value in product class and how they rate one firm's product relative to others. Meanwhile, engineers tear down competitors' products (a tactic known as reverse engineering) in order to understand their performance and technical requirements. Engineering and marketing tests are then incorporated into a product planning matrix that enables the company to evaluate its own product in relation to customers' preferences and competitors' performance. The purpose is to identify areas for improvement and to set targets designed to beat the best of the competition.

An example of such an exercise is found in Figure 4.3. The information shown there refers to an imaginary maker of disposable cigarette lighters, EZ-Lite. This firm has made a comparison of its own product with those of its major

Figure 4.3 Using quality deployment in a mature market

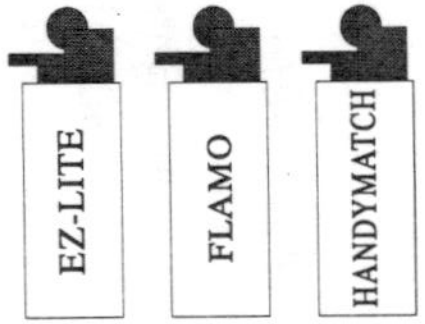

Correlation legend — FUNCTIONAL CHARACTERISTICS: very strong ▲ | strong ■ | possible ○

| | CUSTOMER'S IMPORTANCE RATING (5=highest) | Fluid: % of butane / volume | Maximum flame (height in cms) | Flint mechanism | Size (length in cms) | EZ-LITE (now) | FLAMO | HANDYMATCH | EZ-LITE (target) | MARKET PRICE (in $) | MARKET SHARE (in %) | PROFIT (per unit) |
|---|---|---|---|---|---|---|---|---|---|---|---|---|
| **CUSTOMER'S DEMANDS** | | | | | | *(CUSTOMER SATISFACTION, Scale: 1 to 5, 5=best)* | | | | | | |
| Long service | 5 | ▲ | ○ | ■ | | 3 | 4 | 5 | 5 | | | |
| Reliability | 5 | ○ | | ▲ | | 3 | 4 | 5 | 5 | | | |
| Adjustable flame | 3 | | ▲ | | | 5 | 4 | 4 | 5 | | | |
| Small and compact | 2 | | | | ▲ | 2 | 4 | 4 | 3 | | | |
| **BENCHMARKS** | | | | | | | | | | | | |
| EZ-LITE (now) | | 100% / 5mls | 7cms | Standard | 6cms | | | | | 1.00 | 18 | 9 |
| FLAMO | | 85% / 4mls | 5cms | Standard | 5cms | | | | | 1.10 | 24 | 11 |
| HANDYMATCH | | 80% / 4mls | 5cms | Standard | 5cms | | | | | 1.10 | 33 | 13 |
| EZ-LITE (target) | | 75% / 5mls | 7cms | Standard | 6cms | | | | | 1.10 | 35 | 14 |

HANDYMATCH  FLAMO  EZ-LITE

Source: UNIDO.

rivals (Flamo and Handymatch). First, a representative group of customers was interviewed and asked to indicate the product characteristics they value most.[6] The most frequently cited characteristics were: long service, reliability, an easily adjustable flame height, and a small, compact size. Customers were then asked to rate each of these characteristics. EZ-Lite received a low rating in the two most important categories (long service and reliability).

Armed with this information, EZ-Lite's engineers isolated the functional characteristics of disposable lighters that most closely corresponded to customers' demands. Relationships were rated as very strong, strong, and possible. For example, the functional characteristic, 'lighter fluid volume and composition', is very strongly correlated to long service. Engineers then translated each functional characteristic into its technical equivalent and used this data as a benchmark in the product planning matrix. Reverse engineering revealed that EZ-Lite contains more fluid (5 mls) than other lighters and that EZ-Lite is the only one using 100 per cent butane as fluid.

Based on this exercise, managers concluded that the company had lost touch with its customers. The firm had the lowest market share (18 per cent) and had recently launched a new range of lighters with different colours and attractive patterns on the plastic casing. The marketing staff had erroneously assumed that a more attractive lighter would take sales away from rivals. Handymatch, the long-time market leader, already knew colour and design were not important to customers and offered only three basic colours. One result of this exercise was that EZ-Lite scrapped its misguided efforts to improve appearance and turned its attention to other, more important product characteristics.

The quality deployment exercise also revealed crucial areas that needed improvement. For instance, consumers place much value on long service and EZ-Lite was inferior to its rivals in this regard. Testing showed that the mixture of lighter fluids used by the company was more expensive than that in other lighters and burned more quickly, thus reducing the useful life of EZ-Lite's product. An optimal mixture would have a smaller proportion of butane. By making this adjustment, the company cut its costs and dramatically extended the lifetime of its lighters.

The company also lagged behind in another important field, product reliability. EZ-Lite's engineers repeatedly tested the flint and lighting mechanisms of the three products and found them to be virtually identical. Eventually, they concluded that the durability of the flints and lighting mechanisms of all products performed well and outlasted the life of the fluid in all lighters. EZ-Lite returned to the consumers and after some effort found that many confused long service with reliability. If a lighter ran out of fluid quickly, consumers simply assumed that the brand was unreliable and based their impressions of the product on that assumption. This fact impressed EZ-Lite's managers who redoubled their efforts to combat the problem. An earlier suggestion by a customer — to use a clear plastic casing as a visual signal indicating low lighter fluid — was adopted and subsequent ratings of EZ-Lite's reliability were vastly improved.

In conclusion, quality deployment, reverse engineering and product planning matrices can be an invaluable part of a company's effort to improve its competitive position. The technique helps a firm to stay abreast of customers' preferences and to avoid product designs which do not satisfy these preferences. Quality deployment can be especially effective in mature markets where product characteristics and brand reputation may be more important than price.

## POLICY DEPLOYMENT

Incremental improvements percolate up from the shop floor of the CIF, but strategic planning is the responsibility of executives and filters down through the ranks. Managers can make use of a technique known as policy deployment (PD) to achieve this goal. The process begins with a reassessment of medium and long-range plans for improvement. These plans may refer to any number of areas such as profitability, cost, quality and delivery, and will be defined over a period of time ranging from one to ten years. PD succeeds by first translating this strategic vision into quantifiable goals and tangible plans for each department or function. The results are then passed down through the ranks in the form of annual PD plans.

Managers and workers at each level of the organization assign improvement priorities to support the annual plan. Once these priorities have been determined, the tasks necessary to achieve each goal must be identified and agreed upon. The improvement activities of every department should be expressed in terms of measurable changes in production processes. Progress is carefully monitored, data is collected and results are periodically posted around the factory. While each department pursues its own goals, cross-functional teams will coordinate plans across staff areas.

In addition to the annual plans, a general PD plan is given to each departmental manager. It will cover several points such as top management's long-range policy and strategy, results of previous plans and the improvement responsibilities of the department's managers and workers. The departmental head is expected to discuss the general plan with superiors and subordinates. Eventually, everyone in the organization will be aware of at least four or five strategic aims of the firm.

PD audits are usually conducted by departmental heads on a monthly or quarterly basis. When goals are not being met, managers and workers review the data and devise a different approach to the problem. If results exceed the current goals, the reasons for success are identified and eventually incorporated into standard procedures. Top managers will often carry out their own audit once or twice a year. The chief executive remains in touch with supervisors and workers on the shop floor in order to verify their understanding of the PD plan and the improvement process. The insights gathered by managers and executives during these audits are used in the next round of planning.

PD is a means of converting the long-term vision of managers and executives into concerted action at all levels of the firm. Strategic thinking filters down through the firm in terms of increasingly detailed tasks and goals. Importantly, agreement among all participants will have been reached on procedures, timetables and responsibilities, and no one will be assigned a task without also being given the tools and measures to perform it. Each individual becomes an integral part of policy execution with horizontal and vertical flows of information allowing for coordination between units.[7]

Top managers of mass production firms are just as concerned with strategic management as their counterparts in a CIF, but there are key differences in the way the two groups implement their ideas. For instance, in many mass production firms top executives are the only ones engaged in strategic planning. Subordinates are not invited to participate and suggestions may be seen as a violation of their responsibility. Nor do lower-level managers and workers get the opportunity to participate in the planning process. The lack of communication will be apparent when executives adopt goals like 'zero defects', or 'team work'. Workers and middle managers are unlikely to receive guidance about how to achieve these aims; not surprisingly, the results are often disappointing.

## TEAMS AND GROUPS

Small groups and teams become more important as a manufacturer gains experience in continuous improvement.[8] Firms that are novices in this field will have other concerns — notably, training and the simplification of production processes — but for those with considerable expertise in CITs, the creation of multi-skilled teams offers several advantages. By bringing together workers from different staff areas, the firm builds up a broader, cross-functional perspective among participants. Teams include staff with long experience as well as relatively new employees, a mixture which encourages the transmission of valuable experience and informal information.[9]

The best-known method of teamwork is the quality control circle (QCC). A typical QCC will include no more than ten volunteers, along with a supervisor who serves as group leader. These groups can sometimes determine which objectives to pursue and usually have the authority to enact any changes they propose. Such freedom helps to strengthen the team members' dedication and willingness to collaborate.

QCCs have had their greatest successes in Japan, but many analysts are uncertain that similar results can be achieved elsewhere. Some argue that the QCCs rely on a consensual approach to decision-making which is unique to Japan. Others see these groups as a form of grass-roots involvement where the worker is the main source of most improvements and one of the primary responsibilities of a manager is to encourage worker creativity and effort. Such a management style may be alien to some cultures. A more positive interpretation is offered by other investigators. They see the method as a potent form of worker democracy and employee involvement. With careful planning and preparation, the technique should be transferable from one country to another.

Given this mixture of opinions and assessments, it is not surprising that there is some confusion about the role QCCs should play in a programme of continuous improvement. Many managers assume that formation of these groups will automatically provide an 'injection' of continuous improvement. The danger with this view is that once the groups are established, they are left to operate without managerial support. They frequently become just one more compartmentalized activity to which top managers delegate the responsibility for improvement. A more successful outcome can be realized when managers demonstrate an active interest in the work of QCCs and provide the required resources and support, but make clear that the group has its own agenda and responsibilities.

Another potential source of difficulty is that the concept of QCCs is based on a view of workers' responsibilities that is unfamiliar to managers. They frequently assume that production problems can invariably be attributed to the actions of individuals. However, the performance of workers is conditioned by the production system in which they work. The search for improvements by the QCC focuses on this system and the production processes it encompasses. Teams are expected to gather relevant data and facts upon which to base decisions rather than rely on the subjective impressions about individuals.[10]

Other problems can result from poor planning and lack of preparation when the firm first establishes QCCs. These difficulties can be avoided, or at least minimized, if several preparatory steps are taken:

- The significance of QCCs should be fully understood and supported by top management. The groups have considerable autonomy, but still depend on guidance and support from above. This support is understood in Japanese firms, but is frequently lacking in other industrialized countries where the failure rate for QCC programmes is high (see Hill, 1991, pp. 541–68).

- Firms having no previous experience with QCCs should begin with introductory seminars and conferences. These should be attended by top managers, technical personnel and selected supervisors and clearly spell out the firm's goals for the programme.

- The first QCCs should be composed solely of supervisors. They can gain valuable experience, while demonstrating to workers that management is serious about QCCs. The QCCs can be reconstituted later with supervisors as leaders.

- The groups should use improvement manuals for study and discussion before they move on to concrete ideas about improvements in the plant and its manufacturing processes. Three to six months will be needed before supervisors can assume effective leadership and workers are confident enough to give their opinions freely.

- The effectiveness of QCCs depends on an ongoing programme of training. With experience, team members should be able to determine the main problems, isolate potential causes and identify sources of difficulty. They should also be capable of devising solutions and then retaining the gains which have been made by using modern control methods (Koura, 1972, pp. 16–17).

- Once a solution has been identified and becomes part of standard practice, the QCC should move on to another problem.

In conclusion, QCCs are an invaluable source of progress, but they can never ensure that the firm is a competitive success. The major determinants of higher quality and greater efficiency relate to managerial policy and strategy, design capabilities, vendor relations, and other critical variables that are beyond the influence of supervisors and workers (Juran, 1988, pp. 57–61). Only top management can produce changes in these areas. When significant progress has been made, the prominence of QCCs will diminish. In fact, the approach will eventually be discarded, even in companies where the groups have performed superbly. The leaders in continuous improvement will be able to replace some of the more formal elements of QCCs with more effective routines such as roving improvement teams and frequent meetings on the production line. By that time, the ultimate purpose of the QCCs — to effectively blur the artificial distinction between 'thinking' and 'doing' — will have been achieved.

## TOTAL PRODUCTIVE MAINTENANCE

Like product defects, machine malfunctions adversely affect costs, efficiency and customer satisfaction. In the CIF, machine malfunctions are viewed not as a normal occurrence but as a process breakdown that is preventable. A primary goal is to eliminate malfunctions entirely in order to avoid equipment downtime. This step is necessary before the firm can move on to more streamlined methods of manufacturing and JIT forms of inventory control. Such techniques require that machinery be available on demand, almost continuously (Takahashi and Osada, 1990).

Total productive maintenance (TPM) is the tool used by the CIF to prevent malfunctions.[11] Though it is not always apparent, the performance and condition of machinery directly reflects the behaviour of people in the firm. For example, if a machine suddenly breaks down the immediate cause is usually easy to discover. Suppose a seal ruptures, allowing oil to escape which causes machine damage and interrupts production. At first glance the cause of this malfunction is clear: a ruptured seal. But a manager who follows TPM will not be content with such a simple explanation. A whole series of probing questions are asked before a decision is made about the real cause of the problem (see Box 4.2). Such dogged investigation usually reveals that the true source of the problem is a combination of factors involving not just production-line operators but supervisors or managers as well.

Machinery malfunctions can generally be traced back to one or more of the following causes which TPM is designed to address (see Suzaki, 1987, p. 116):

- poor maintenance of machine requirements, such as sloppy housekeeping, oiling or bolt-tightening;

- failure to maintain correct operating conditions, for example, ignoring abnormal temperatures, noise, speed, vibration or torque;

- low levels of worker skills and training in the proper operation of the machinery, maintenance-crew errors, and the like;

- deterioration of equipment, wearing-down of bearings, gears, fixtures and so on;

**Box 4.2   Identifying the 'true' reasons for machinery breakdowns**

When a machine breakdown or some other problem occurs, investigators in the CIF often ask 'why' five times. In this way the ultimate causes of problems can be better revealed.

Problem:  A broken seal

1)   **Why** did the seal break?  There were fine cracks in the seal.

2)   **Why** was the seal cracked?  It was overdue for replacement.

3)   **Why** was the seal not replaced on time?  The operators did not alert the maintenance crew.

4)   **Why** did the operators not alert the maintenance crew?  The supervisor told the operators to forget about maintenance and keep the machines running.

5)   **Why** did the supervisor tell the operators to ignore the maintenance schedule? The supervisor was told by the production manager to do whatever was required to ensure that the shipment left the factory as scheduled.

- poorly designed machines or processes.

TPM derives from the premise that machine problems are caused by people and those who use the equipment should have the primary responsibility for maintenance. Operators are trained to maintain normal operating conditions, to perform routine preventive maintenance, to inspect their machines daily, to clean their machines on a routine basis, and even to perform basic repairs.[12] This training helps workers to identify the early signs of trouble. They learn about odd noises, speeds, odours and so forth that can signal impending problems. TPM teams made up of operators and maintenance personnel will discuss hypothetical problems that can arise, ways of identifying these problems and actions designed to eliminate them.

Operators are expected to carry out a daily programme of equipment inspections which includes routine cleaning and careful observation to detect any obvious leaks or noises.[13] In some plants 'machine handkerchiefs' are used to wipe down the machinery. This practice reveals leaks, cracks, blown seals and other problems before they cause trouble. Cleaning and inspection of machines by operators are the two most important activities for discovering abnormal conditions.

Firms embarking on a programme of TPM will typically proceed through four basic phases of machine maintenance. Early in the first phase, managers and operators encounter the legacy of neglect due to poor maintenance practices. Machines have not been properly oiled, equipment is not correctly adjusted, parts are dangerously worn, and bolts need tightening.[14] Machines need to be cleaned and a routine of basic maintenance procedures for operators should be installed. Work may also be needed to restore the machinery to its original level of performance. In the second phase, machines are operated under prescribed conditions and subject only to normal wear and tear. Regular preventive maintenance begins to yield the benefits of sharply reduced downtime. In the third phase, efforts to maintain machines in optimal operating condition are conducted on a continuous basis and include the intervention of operators to prevent abnormal conditions. Operators will be able to repair many problems themselves. Visual aids are used to show proper equipment settings and operating practices. Lines can be painted on the machines indicating the correct position for tightened bolts and other simple instructions. Simple devices are placed on machines to prevent their use unless proper procedures are being followed. Certain parts may even be redesigned or modified to extend a machine's life. In the fourth phase the condition of machinery is constantly monitored by operators. The purpose is to ensure that timely maintenance is performed and that information is available on the time lost due to set-ups, machinery adjustments, poor yields and defectives (see Box 4.3). Diagnostic equipment is used to forecast the life of machine parts and the quality of the product. Many plants employ in-house personnel to design and manufacture equipment and parts which will increase machine efficiency. All these tasks are supported by a circular flow of information among machine operators, machine designers and managers. These teams use various tools of continuous improvement, such as the 5-S movement, graphs and statistical methods to devise new ways of improving equipment performance.

## JUST-IN-TIME MANUFACTURING

One of the most powerful technologies to be perfected by practitioners of continuous improvement is just-in-time manufacturing (JIT).[15] Developed by Toyota Motors, the technology is the outcome of more than 30 years of work and experimentation. The original purpose was to eliminate the build-up of inventories of work-in-process (WIP) but the modern version of JIT is more ambitious. It has evolved into a highly sophisticated exercise, requiring coordination between several different techniques and methods.

---

**Box 4.3   Monitoring the effectiveness of machinery and equipment**

As the firm becomes more experienced, the goals of its maintenance programme will be extended to maximize the operating time of machinery. In this more comprehensive form, TPM has led to various measures of machine effectiveness. One is the idea of a 'theoretical cycle time' which assumes that the set-up is done very quickly (usually in 10 minutes or less). Another is the actual cycle time which includes run time and actual set-up time. These indicators are used in combination to determine the effectiveness of equipment as shown below. By assuming such a short theoretical cycle time, the measurement is extremely rigorous (see Rodriguez, 1992, pp. 155–6):

$$\text{Equipment effectiveness} = \text{Machine availability} \times \text{Performance efficiency} \times \text{Rate of quality}$$

$$= \frac{\text{Planned time} - \text{down-time}}{\text{Planned time}} \times \frac{\text{Theoretical cycle time}}{\text{Actual cycle time}} \times \frac{\text{Good parts}}{\text{Parts produced}}$$

Since the 1970s firms in industrialized countries have competed for a preventive maintenance prize. Japan's recent winners have had equipment effectiveness ratios of over 85 per cent. The best plants in the United States usually report ratios of around 70 per cent, while the average in that country is 25–30 per cent.

---

Though it has attracted great interest, the goal of JIT manufacturing has proven to be elusive. There are several reasons for disappointment. First, success often requires that the firm alter its structure and organizational form but managers are reluctant to do this (see Chapter 3). Second, many would-be users focus only on JIT's more obvious and easily replicated features (for example, the plant layout and machinery) while ignoring the softer forms of technology described in this chapter. Yet the latter are essential if the dies, jigs, self-stopping machinery and other 'hard technologies' are to function properly. Third, some managers assume that JIT is a method of inventory control and nothing more. That view leads them to place great emphasis on certain elements of the technique but ignore others. These firms usually manage to reduce inventories, though many of the other benefits of JIT will be forgone. Finally, managers may expect JIT to provide a significant measure of 'production flexibility', meaning that their plants can shift quickly and cheaply from one product model to another and profitably operate at moderate (rather than high) rates of capacity utilization. In fact, a firm must already have such capabilities before it attempts to introduce this technology. JIT will not create production- flexibility; and without it, the firm can never maximize the benefits of this procedure.

The drive to achieve production flexibility can be thwarted by a breakdown or unsynchronized operations in any part of the manufacturing system. Some of the more common obstacles have been noted by Takahashi and Osada (1990, pp. 14–15). They include:

- long staging or set-up times for changeovers which lead to a build-up of WIP inventories and force interruptions in work further down the production line;

- variations in the capabilities of different work centres which cause WIP to accumulate at various points in the production line;

- an imbalance in the work loads of two consecutive operations which inflates inventories or disrupts subsequent operations;

- a high number of defects in one operation which disrupts subsequent operations or requires a buffer stock for components and parts;

- frequent equipment breakdowns and long repair times;

- high rates of absenteeism and personnel turnover;

- unsafe equipment or other practices that have a negative impact on the flow of production.

What are the most important circumstances which must exist if obstacles such as these are to be avoided? They include: (i) abbreviated changeover times and defect-free production lines; (ii) production methods which are 'lean' and discourage inventory build-up; (iii) an effective system of inventory control; and (iv) a close working relationship with suppliers. These conditions are prerequisites for a comprehensive and fully effective system of JIT manufacturing and are discussed below.

## Reducing Changeover Times and Defects

The insistence that set-ups and changeovers be carried out swiftly stems from the need to maximize process efficiency. That concept takes into account both the time spent working on materials and the time materials are in the production system but no value is being added. When machinery set-ups and changeovers are lengthy, process efficiency is reduced. Quick changeovers not only prevent inventory build-up but smooth out the production runs of suppliers, making them more process-efficient. Such a view is alien to many mass producers where changeover costs are treated as unavoidable. Accordingly, the latter firms opt for long production runs in order to maximize operational efficiency (for example productivity per worker or per machine). This tactic minimizes the need for changeovers, though it generates non-production costs. Long production runs are operationally efficient, but are process-inefficient.

Along with reduced changeover times, the firm must ensure that production is free of defects. One way to ensure that defects do not impede production is to install machinery that automatically shuts down before defects are produced.[16] Such machines are neither expensive nor complex, and offer several advantages. Their installation allows the firm to develop U-shaped multi-machining areas which are attended by only one operator. That configuration is superior to the straight-line layout favoured by mass manufacturers which require one person per machine. The result is a large increase in labour productivity that is not necessarily based on harder or faster work but on organizational innovation. Workers and supervisors also have more time and energy to solve problems and search for improvements.

These two goals, abbreviated changeover times and defect-free production, loom especially important in today's markets where demand can shift rapidly and customers are increasingly discriminating. Because it can quickly shift from production of one product model to another without incurring large costs, the JIT manufacturer is better able to accommodate customers' preferences. And by relying on small and inexpensive machines, it is capable of operating at less than full capacity. The results are a reduction in total production time and shorter production runs. These savings outweigh the costs incurred when inexpensive machinery stands still.

## Rigorous Systems of Production Control

By organizing itself to achieve operational efficiency, the mass producer encounters problems whenever customers' preferences shift unexpectedly or demand contracts. These firms depend on a 'push system' of production which moves parts and materials along a production line as workers wait to perform the next step. Conveyor belts determine the pace of work in plants designed to accommodate large and expensive machines that speed throughput over long and relatively predictable production runs. Managers strive to balance the distribution of work along the production line in order to maintain a continuous flow but precision is rarely achieved. Costly buffer stocks accumulate at each production stage. The uncertainty of demand and the need to operate near full capacity lead the mass producer to produce large quantities of finished products 'just in case' (see Drummond, 1992, pp. 120–25).

In contrast to the mass producer's push system, JIT 'pulls' material down the production line. Items are produced only when they are required by the following step in the process. Operators signal their readiness for new material and so avoid the accumulation of WIP. With no WIP or buffer stocks, a defective part can not be replaced and the operator must stop the production line. The work site and operator responsible for the defect are identified and immediately alerted to the problem because the production line comes to a standstill. Such a system clearly requires rigorous control over manufacturing processes and quality, as well as the underlying levels of variation (see Box 4.4).

**Effective Systems of Inventory Control**

JIT manufacturing is based on stringent methods of inventory control. One of the most popular is the Japanese version known as 'kanban', which means 'visible record' or 'visible plate'. First developed by engineers in Toyota Motors, kanban is not just a powerful form of inventory control but also a catalyst for discovering improvement opportunities. Kanban cards act as a visual source of information for inventory control, production volume and other data. Typically, there will be a special container designed to hold a small quantity of every component used by operators. For each container there are two kanban cards which list part numbers, container capacities and other facts. One card serves the work centre which produces the parts while the other is for the operators who handle them. When a container is empty, the kanban card is returned to the source of supply where it acts as a visual pull-signal.

Kanban systems will be different, though most firms adhere to a basic set of rules. First, operators can only obtain parts from an upstream process that is identified and described on the attached kanban card. This requirement imposes the discipline necessary to achieve the smooth flow of parts and

---

**Box 4.4    Applicability of 'pull systems' of production control**

Several pre-conditions for successful installation of a pull system are noted in the text. In addition, such systems may not be appropriate in all cases. First, a portion of a firm's production must involve the manufacture of identical or highly similar product groups. Pull systems could then be used to make these components or items, though not others produced by the firm. Second, it must be economically advantageous for the firm to operate a set of machines dedicated to these types of repetitive operations. Production cells relying on pull systems can then be set up to produce those components, parts or products which satisfy these requirements (Ray, 1992, pp. 181–90).

material. Second, operators can only produce those parts requested by kanban by downstream users. Finally, to eliminate unnecessary overproduction and time, no materials can be requested or produced without a kanban card.

The number of kanban cards is carefully monitored by management; too many cards may indicate a wasteful build-up of inventories. Managers will also gradually reduce the number of cards in circulation, hoping to expose waste and more tightly link the production process. The tactic, which amounts to the intentional creation of problems, is an effective way to identify wasteful practices that can be eliminated or redesigned to reduce time spent in storage, transport, or production.[17]

### Close Links with Suppliers

Many disruptions to the smooth flow of production lines may originate with external suppliers. Close contacts with these suppliers are essential if JIT manufacturing is to succeed. The boundaries separating the manufacturer from its suppliers gradually become blurred through cooperative arrangements in design, process control, R&D, cost reduction and training. Production teams often include representatives of different firms in the supply chain.

The demands placed on suppliers can be considerable. They are expected to deliver precise numbers of components, parts or materials to a designated point of use. These deliveries must be frequent and always in small quantities. Suppliers must also satisfy rigorous quality specifications so there is no need to inspect incoming materials. JIT manufacturers work closely with their suppliers to meet these goals but few have been able to maintain such tight relationships for an extended period of time.

The requirements of JIT manufacturing eventually take a toll, creating strains between buyers and suppliers. When a manufacturer dominates a particular market, it is able to dictate to suppliers, but this tactic does little to encourage the long-term cooperation which JIT requires. If buyers choose to implement the method coercively, suppliers will resent what they see as interference or ruthless price bargaining. Another common complaint of suppliers is that they must bear the cost of having to deliver small amounts at frequent intervals. Frequently, suppliers will simply be unwilling to go through the effort to improve. Such disputes are evidence that there has not been adequate communication and preparation between the customer and supplier.[18]

In conclusion, JIT manufacturing is vulnerable to supply interruptions and failures but it has also established the use of time as a key competitive metric. It is not an option to be considered by the new practitioners of continuous improvement. However, for the experienced firm which has already attained a high degree of production flexibility through organizational innovations and improvement, JIT is a valuable means of achieving competitive superiority. More than any other technique, it dramatically demonstrates that improved process and product performance can occur simultaneously with reduced cost and greater flexibility.

## NOTES

1. Also known as the Shewhart cycle and the Deming wheel, there are several versions of this tool. A slightly different application calls for the firm to establish a standard for the product or process before considering its options for improvement.

2. This idea has a long history. Henry Ford discussed this concept at length during the 1920s and his writings on the subject were intensely studied by Japanese automobile manufacturers (Suzaki, 1987, p. 10).

3. In assembly operations, a defective component can require the complete disassembly of the product with additional parts being needed to complete the product.

4. The 5-S movement takes its name from the initials of five Japanese words: *seiri* (straighten up); *seiton* (put things in order); *seiso* (clean up); *seiketsu* (overall cleanliness); and *shitsuke* (discipline).

5. In addition to its other distinguishing characteristics, QD places a high priority on information exchange between the various groups involved in projects. The conventional approach to product development assumes that customers will indicate their preferences to the marketing department where these are analysed and then relayed to those responsible for design engineering. The latter group designs the product and passes it on to the manufacturing department which is expected to make it. The conventional approach allows few opportunities for information exchange.

6. A representative group should include pipe smokers, cigarette smokers, and customers who use lighters for barbecue grills, fireplaces or gas burners. Each group would have slightly different product requirements.

7. The reader should not confuse the idea of policy deployment with the rival approach of management by objective, which is discussed in Chapter 3.

8. Because many of these firms are already experienced practitioners of CIT, the teams and groups they establish will be employed to fine-tune a production system that is already running smoothly.

9. In several countries employees come from different ethnic, religious, tribal and socioeconomic backgrounds. A history of antagonism between different groups can often be observed in the workplace and is inimical to continuous improvement. In addition to the normal benefits, group work may contribute to the lessening of tension and increase group cohesion.

10. The CIF will already have provided ample training which enables the team to identify the main problems, isolate the potential causes, and then identify the real source of difficulty. Team members are capable of devising solutions and then retaining the gains which have been made by using modern control methods (Koura, 1972, pp. 16–17).

11. Similar programmes have been referred to as Total Preventive Maintenance.

12. The operator's daily regime begins with a thorough personal examination of the equipment. There may be a detailed check-list to go through to ensure that the equipment does not fail during the day. Such a routine is similar to the double-checking of aircraft done by commercial aviation. In fact, CIFs often refer to the extremely low number of critical machine failures in the airline industry as a goal worth copying on the shop floor. This idea is unfamiliar to many mass producers who assume that machines breakdowns are a normal part of the manufacturing system. The use of buffer stocks is justified by that interpretation (Schonberger, 1982, pp. 136–7).

13. A worker's machine often has a sign with his name on it which signifies responsibility for basic inspections and maintenance.

14. The significance of simple activities such as bolt-tightening can not be underestimated. One firm in Japan found that by re-tightening tens of thousands of bolts, one at a time, then machine breakdowns were reduced by 80 per cent (Suzaki, 1987, p. 119).

15. This technology goes by several names which are used interchangeably. Other examples are: pull systems; stock-less manufacturing and kanban. Various techniques like cellular manufacturing, balanced production operations and JIT delivery offer a path to JIT forms of manufacturing.

16. Such machines were invented by Sakichi Toyoda in the early years of the twentieth century. Toyota began as a textile loom company and became successful because of the automatic self-stopping loom which revolutionized weaving (Nayak and Ketteringham, 1986, p. 217).

17 The kanban system and other methods described here can be effectively supplemented by simple methods of mistake-proofing, known in Japanese as 'pokayoke'. There are thousands of such simple examples of pokayoke improvements — such as designing parts so that they can only be assembled the correct way, or the design of a storage device that eliminates miscounts by only allowing the storage of the correct number of parts (Huge, 1992, p. 149). Many of the most effective pokayoke improvements come from workers and their immediate supervisors. The quality control circle has been a prime source of this kind of production-line improvement. Pokayoke is an effective way of aiding the flow of non-defective parts that is required by JIT.

18 In many parts of the world the rudimentary state of manufacturing and the lack of basic infrastructure makes JIT manufacturing exceedingly difficult.

# 5. The Statistical Tools

The process of continuous improvement involves a countless number of tiny adaptations or innovations in daily operations. These modifications are an invaluable source of competitive strength, but they can not be undertaken haphazardly. Some framework is needed to identify the truly important areas which need improvement, to separate the essential from the not-so-essential, and to ensure that adaptations do not have contradictory effects. A number of statistical tools and methods exist for this purpose and are discussed in this chapter. They provide the objectivity needed to ensure that progress is genuine and lasting.

Many plants will have statistical charts and graphs hanging from every machine as well as posters exhorting workers to increase quality and reduce defects. These may leave the impression that quality and improvement are overriding goals of the firm. But all too often, senior managers delegate their responsibilities to subordinates, doing little or nothing to improve the production system. By themselves, engineers can not sustain a programme for continuous improvement in products and processes; nor will the workforce receive the direction and guidance they require. In these circumstances statistical methods more closely resemble a form of damage control rather than a means of continuous improvement.

Without the active involvement of senior managers, programmes for continuous improvement may actually have negative consequences. Many employees immediately assume that the firm is not really committed to these goals. Line workers lacking training in basic statistical methods tend to regard the charts and statistical methods as just another form of work appraisal, as a means of eliminating workers, or an effort to get more from each employee. In some cases they are right. Many supporters of quality control and programmes for continuous improvement have become disenchanted, mistakenly concluding that the methods themselves are ineffective or oversold. The negative reactions voiced about programmes for total quality control (TQC) and the like may be traceable to such misapplications.

The statistical tools described here are a crucial part of the day-to-day operations of firms in industrialized countries. The same sorts of programmes have yet to be adopted by many manufacturers in developing countries. Yet these statistical tools may be especially suitable for factories in that part of the world since they do not require new equipment or substantial investments.

Indeed, this is one of the main reasons why Japanese manufacturers were so quick to introduce statistical procedures following the Second World War. Japanese experts realized that statistical quality control was an effective way of upgrading process performance and product quality without huge spending on new equipment (Mann, 1989, p.16). Many firms in developing countries find themselves in a similar situation today. They lack the finances to enlarge, modernize or automate their operations, but they can still make great strides through effective use of statistical methods.

This chapter provides a general introduction to statistical process control (SPC). The presentation is aimed at readers with little or no statistical training, though it is not intended to be a primer on SPC. Its purpose is merely to demonstrate how these tools are used and what they are supposed to accomplish. Ultimately, the firm's workforce (including management) will require formal training in these methods, if they are to be applied in day-to-day work.

## MONITORING VARIATION IN MANUFACTURING PROCESSES

The statistical tools at the manager's disposal are intended to help him deal with the ubiquitous problem of variation. The theoretical goal is total elimination of variation from all manufacturing processes and operations carried out by the firm. In a practical sense that objective will never be reached. Successful implementors of CIT will doggedly pursue this elusive standard nonetheless, confident in the knowledge that a constant stream of minor improvements will ensure their firm's ability to compete with all rivals.

Variation is the result of a complex interaction between workers, procedures, materials and equipment. And it can exist within any part of a production system. The first step in the monitoring exercise is to distinguish between two broadly different types of variation. Both were defined and described in Chapter 1 but it is useful to revisit these ideas here. The first, known as *common-cause* variation, is attributable to any sources that are common to the manufacturing system (see Figure 1.1). These disturbances affect every part of the manufacturing system and will persist until remedies are found. Variation can also be due to *special causes*. Unlike common sources of variability, the latter types of disturbances occur only intermittently. They may be attributed to worker behaviour, methods of operation or equipment variations. Whatever the reason, special causes are due to events that are beyond the firm's usual experience.

When both common and special causes exist, the situation is confused. The amount of variation in the manufacturing system or process is not predictable;

nor is the proportion of unacceptable or defective outcomes. In such a case the operation is regarded as 'out of control'. The first priority is to eliminate special causes of variation. Once this is done, the system is said to be 'in control', meaning that it is subject only to common causes of variation. Such a condition is still far from the ideal — in fact, performance may continue to be erratic, unreliable or wasteful. The distinction is important nonetheless. The actual process of continuous improvement can not begin until special causes have been eliminated and the system is in control.

Definitions of the two causes of variation are clear enough but in practice it can be hard to distinguish one from the other. One danger is that managers rely on casual inference to identify the cause of problems. In that case, most deviations — for example, a defective product or inferior performance in a particular manufacturing process — tend to be treated as one-time occurrences. Such an approach makes no distinction between common and special causes, leaving the manager with few clues about where to search for the underlying problem. Another source of confusion is the tendency of managers to adopt a pragmatic approach, focusing attention on specific manufacturing processes or outcomes. In fact, the philosophy of continuous improvement stipulates that the search for sources of variation extend to all parts of the production system. The piecemeal approach of many managers is often translated into the use of numerical standards to measure performance. Standards may be set for various purposes. For example, they may specify output goals, define the results of 'best practice' or determine the ideal level of effort and performance.

Figure 5.1 illustrates how inappropriately constructed standards of perfor- mance lead to erroneous conclusions. Standard A represents the firm's best guess of output per worker hour among the industry's leaders. Attempts to match this standard could have disastrous results for the firm if the real reasons for fluctuations in labour productivity are not first addressed. Similarly, standard B is based on the firm's own figures for output per worker hour and may be set too low. The results of incorrect performance standards can lead to managerial complacency and poor worker morale.

If managers have little idea about the statistical stability of a manufacturing process, the adoption of inappropriate numerical standards can divert attention from more critical problems. Even worse, such standards can have a negative impact on costs in several ways:

- they can lead to wasteful types of remedial action or fail to address the true source of problems;

- they may contribute to a deterioration in the quality of output and lead to the stagnation of employees' skills;

*Figure 5.1   Measuring variation by numerical standards*

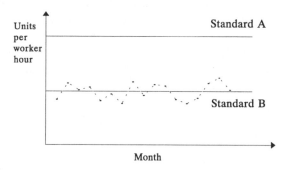

- they can result in conditions where maintenance of machinery and equipment is neglected or where cooperation between different parts of the organization is jeopardized.

One example of these negative consequences arises when inappropriate targets for throughput are adopted. In such a case operators may be inclined to release material of poor quality simply to boost their output. Throughput would rise, but the actual yield could still fall as defects and rework escalate. The true costs of this misjudgement are even greater when defective or low-quality items are sold to customers. Less obvious are the opportunities forgone because inappropriate standards focus workers' attention not on improving productivity but on meeting short-term production targets.

Similar dangers exist when operators choose to run machinery without adequate maintenance. In order to meet or exceed their quota, workers on one shift will be tempted to defer maintenance and exhaust all work-in-progress. Those on the following shift then face a longer and more complicated start-up and greater down-time for maintenance. These problems are compounded if managers choose to treat each work shift as an independent competitor, pitting one group against another to spur higher production.

In general, management's failure to adopt a very broad or system-wide perspective reduces workers' incentives to share knowledge and to ensure the smooth transfer of responsibilities across shifts and departments. Organizations that do not capitalize upon the enormous reservoir of creative ability and production knowledge of workers and engineers squander their opportunities to improve. Ironically, if managers were to utilize their machinery as inefficiently as they handle their staff, they would be regarded as grossly negligent.

# IDENTIFYING SOURCES OF VARIATION

The types of problems discussed above will occur when managers know very little about the critical characteristics of their manufacturing processes and production systems. Yet there are several simple tools which can help them identify the causes of variation and obtain a better understanding of their systems. Five of these tools are discussed here:

- process flow charts
- check sheets
- Pareto diagrams
- cause-and-effect diagrams
- histograms

## Process Flow Charts

The search for sources of variation often begins by outlining the sequence of steps occurring in a particular manufacturing processes. Process flow charts serve this purpose. They can be used to: (i) identify unnecessary or wasteful steps in the process, (ii) convey a clear picture of workers' responsibilities and their impact on the process, and (iii) provide a framework for discussion of key issues which can later be resolved by the workers themselves. In fact, a series of charts are usually required to capture all the kinds of process information required. As work proceeds, these are updated and more detail is added (see Box 5.1).

Construction of a process flow chart can proceed according to the following steps:

- **Determine the process boundaries**. The first step is to identify the beginning and end of the manufacturing process, along with all the associated inputs and outputs. Next, the different departments and functions involved in each process step must be determined.

- **Create a flow chart for the process**. Using information gathered from managers, engineers, supervisors and line personnel, a chart showing the sequence of steps in the process is constructed. Even at this early stage, it will be critical to see how workers from different shifts and departments view the overall process. Such shared information is fertile ground for continuous improvement. The first version of the chart tends to be fairly general but gradually more details are added. As work proceeds, different departments create their own versions of the chart.

**Box 5.1   Creating a flow chart: the symbols and their meaning**

Because most charts are complicated to decipher, analysts try to limit themselves to a few simple symbols. Any production system will include several manufacturing processes, the boundaries of which are denoted by an oval-shaped symbol. Within each manufacturing process, several different steps will be required such as heating, filling containers or spraying. Each of these steps would be represented by a rectangular symbol. Finally, certain decisions must be made during the course of a manufacturing process. For example, is an item defective and is rework needed? Decisions are identified by the diamond-shaped symbol shown below.

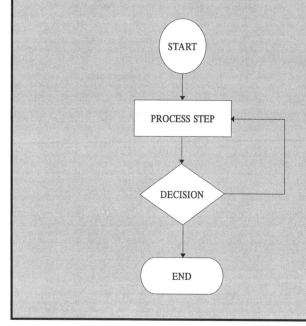

These can be compared in order to identify opportunities for co-ordination and other improvements.

- **Confirm the accuracy of the flow chart**. Once the chart is completed, workers should be consulted regarding their opinions about the changes needed. This dialogue must be constantly repeated — a practice which recognizes that the firm's workforce is the only asset that truly generates change and improvement.

- **Tailor the flow chart to the needs of the users**. Each group of workers requires information at a different level of detail.[1] Several versions of the process flow chart will eventually have to be prepared to ensure that every set of users gets the information they need to improve the process.

A simplified version of a process flow chart is shown in Figure 5.2. The chart, which describes the process of assembling hornpads found in the steering wheels of cars, is preliminary and incomplete. For example, it incorporates no decision points, although operators would be expected to identify defective items and decide whether these items should be scrapped or reworked. It follows that later versions of this flow chart would have to be more comprehensive and detailed. Eventually, the charts become very complex. For more realistic examples and further discussion, the reader should consult the appendix.

## Check Sheets

Flow charts indicate where problems exist and common causes of variation are likely to be encountered. Once these features have been identified, more detailed data on each specific step in the manufacturing process is collected on check sheets for later use in statistical process control. Also known as data collection sheets, these show the lot numbers for incoming raw materials, machine numbers, parts numbers and the like. Other information such as temperature changes, maintenance procedures, adjustments to machines or line stops may also be included since this, too, can reveal sources of variation. Finally, the sheets indicate the time when data was recorded, the names of those completing the check sheets, and any other information on new conditions affecting the process. The format of these check sheets will differ depending on the data collected. The example given in Figure 5.3 records the location and types of defects observed in wooden plaques as they come off the assembly line.

*Figure 5.2    Flow diagram for the assembly of hornpads*

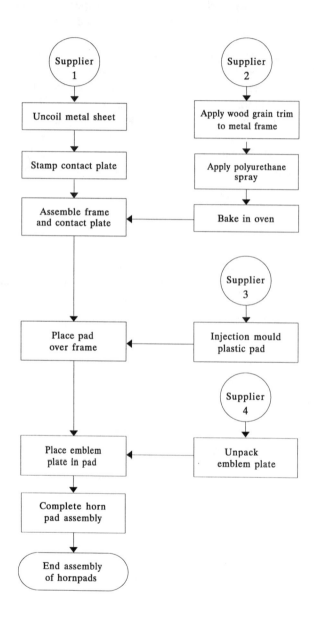

*Figure 5.3    Example of a check sheet to record defects*

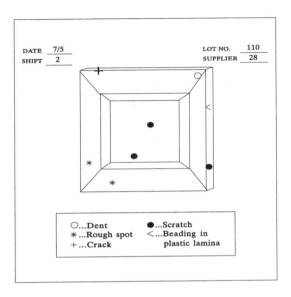

## Pareto Diagrams

As the volume of data being collected grows, analysts will need to determine which sources of statistical variation are the most troublesome. They do this by constructing a Pareto diagram which is essentially a vertical bar graph showing the frequency of events arranged by category and ordered from the largest to the smallest. Variation may be analysed in different ways but one of the more common approaches is to focus on the number of defects. Information of this type is usually obtained by inspecting materials to see if they meet in-house specifications.[2]

Such an application can be illustrated with the help of an earlier example. Suppose, for instance, that 1,000 hornpad assemblies are inspected and the results are recorded on check sheets. This information can then be used to construct a Pareto diagram such as the one in Figure 5.4. A total of 260 assemblies (26 per cent of all inspections) were found to be defective.

*Figure 5.4    Pareto diagram showing occurrence of defects by category*

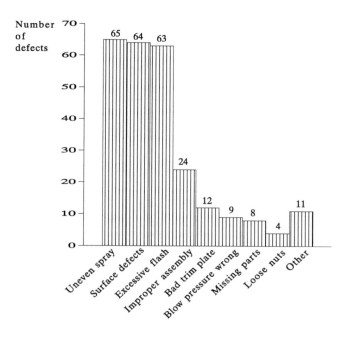

However, three types of defects — uneven spray, surface flaws and excessive flash — account for 74 per cent of all problems. By concentrating their search on these three characteristics, managers will be able to eliminate the majority of defects.

In general, Pareto diagrams identify which defects are most important and help to pinpoint the action needed to avoid them. Unfortunately, these diagrams do not enable us to distinguish between special and common causes. Remedial action to eliminate chronic problems in the production system can not be taken until special causes of variation have been eliminated.

**Cause-and-Effect Diagrams**

An effective tool to help employees organize their ideas and work methods is the cause-and-effect diagram.[3] Employees first agree to study a certain process characteristic (possibly after examining a flow chart). A diagram of this process characteristic or problem, along with the main contributing factors and more detailed factors, is then constructed. Careful study of cause-and-effect diagrams should help the manager answer various questions such as: What is known about the impact of certain causes of the problem at hand? Which of these causes can, or should, be controlled? What types of interactions between causes actually affect the process and the quality characteristics under study? There is no single set of rules or guidelines for construction of a cause-and-effect diagram. One way is to single out the potential causes of a problem. These generally fall into one of the following categories:

- personnel
- materials
- equipment
- production methods
- measurements
- production environment.

Alternatively, the diagram may be designed to link the problem under study to certain functions or departments within the firm. A highly simplified version is presented in Figure 5.5 while a more detailed discussion can be found in the appendix.

*Figure 5.5   Simplified cause-and-effect diagram*

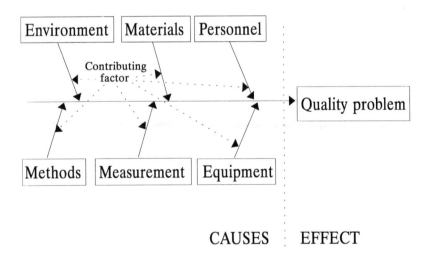

CAUSES    EFFECT

## Histograms

Managers and engineers will often seek information about aspects of quality by studying a sample of items drawn from a larger number of products such as a production lot. Items in the sample will be chosen at random, meaning that each should have an equal probability of selection. Through this means the investigator tries to ensure that the characteristics of the sample are representative of all items being produced. The characteristics identified in the sample can be used to draw inferences about the underlying quality of the product or manufacturing process. As the sampling process is repeated and the amount of data grows, the results become increasingly difficult to evaluate and interpret. To simplify matters, the data can be organized in the form of a histogram which will provide a basic understanding of a population at a glance. Histograms are simply graphs showing the range of measurements on the horizontal axis and the frequency of their occurrence on the vertical axis.

The shape of a histogram can tell us a great deal about the general quality characteristics of product or process.[4] Most common is the mound-shaped or bell-shaped version shown in Figure 5.6. In this case observations tend to be clustered around a centre value and the frequency of their occurrence diminishes as the distance from the centre point increases. The mound-shaped pattern approximates the statistician's notion of a normal distribution. In practice, many histograms will not have this distribution; they come in a variety of shapes and patterns which can often be explained in terms of various manufacturing practices and characteristics (see Box 5.2).

In conclusion, every manufacturing establishment or system, along with each of the manufacturing processes within that system, generates large amounts of information. The five statistical tools we have described here help

*Figure 5.6    Histogram with a normal distribution*

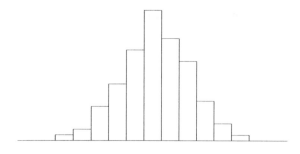

**Box 5.2  Histograms and their underlying distribution**

Histograms come in all shapes and patterns which can often be explained in terms of various manufacturing practices and conditions. One possibility is a 'cliff-shaped' pattern where several categories of events have a similar number of occurrences while others have a much fewer number of occurrences (see below). Such a pattern is familiar to purchasers of materials or parts. Typically, the vendor will not ship items that fail to meet a certain standard, possibly because they do not satisfy buyers' specifications. Thus purchasers observe a sharp drop in the occurrence of values outside the acceptable standard. Other histograms will be skewed to the right or left with a large number of observations at one end of the distribution. This pattern can occur when all materials are subject to screening because of high process variation. Other patterns and shapes will be encountered and the reasons will vary. They may be due to: errors in methods of measurement, the unintentional mixture of two slightly different products or production batches, an abnormality in the manufacturing process and so on. For further discussion of this aspect, see the appendix.

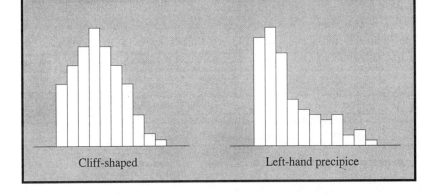

Cliff-shaped                    Left-hand precipice

managers and engineers use that data to determine the sources of variation and to make some judgements about effects.

## COLLECTING AND COMPILING THE DATA

The foregoing section considered various means of organizing and displaying data but nothing has been said about the methods of data collection. The importance of this phase should not be underestimated since it will determine the reliability of the statistical results.

A large number of observations are generally needed to obtain an accurate picture of variation and it is not practical that each of these is shown individually in the charts and graphs that are constructed. Instead, several observations are treated as part of a 'subgroup' and only the average value for each subgroup is considered. For example, a firm may decide to study one of its manufacturing processes by taking ten measurements on a certain characteristic during each production day. The data collected each day can be treated as a subgroup and the daily averages would be used in the ensuing analysis. Subgroups can also be defined by production hour, by lot, by number of defects per product or in other ways.

The definition of a subgroup in the example used here is straightforward but that is not always the case. If their results are to be accurate, investigators must be sure that each subgroup contains a set of *comparable* items. This requirement often leads them to create subgroups from 'production lots'. The assumption behind this approach is that all items in each production lot will have been manufactured under similar conditions. Those which are selected at random from the production lot to make up a subgroup will satisfy the criterion of comparability. Accordingly, a production lot is regarded as a group of like items produced under common causes (see Box 5.3).

In practice, there are several guidelines to ensure that the items in a production lot (and in the corresponding subgroup) are all comparable. The

---

**Box 5.3    What is meant by a 'production lot'?**

A production lot can be defined as a group of like items produced by a manufacturing system subject only to common causes of variation. Accordingly, each item in a lot should possess a high degree of uniformity. In its simplest form, a lot can be obtained from a single machine run by a single operator. A portion of the items found in a factory would satisfy this definition, though many manufacturing operations give rise to product mixtures. These may be made from different batches of inputs, produced on different machines or with different operators. Eventually, all the items may be dumped into a common container and treated as a production lot, even though they are really a mixture. Confusion can also arise when the manufacturing process is continuous and common to all items but the input materials are not. In such circumstances production lots are usually determined by the size of the production run or by the amount produced in a given period of time (output per shift or per week).

For product acceptance decisions, it is important that items be kept in separated lots identified by common causes of production. Such a practice is known as 'preserving the order' and will be very helpful when drawing up subgroups to be used in the construction of control charts. In processes which exhibit a time-to-time variation (for example, chemical solutions that change very slowly or tools that gradually wear), preservation of the order is accomplished by maintaining the time sequence in which various portions of the lot were made. Without such an arrangement, valuable knowledge about the conditions under which the product was made is lost (see Juran and Cook, 1974).

most common methods of ensuring comparability are to define production lots in one of the following ways:

- according to the suspected causes of variation;

- by dividing production into equal quantities of items produced or into lots produced during equal time intervals; or

- by ignoring the practice of creating production lots and simply selecting subgroups directly from the manufacturing process.

The first of these methods is appropriate if managers suspect that a particular machine is the source of substantial variation. A valid test would be to compare the material supplied by this particular piece of equipment with that obtained from similar machines in the production line. Items produced by the suspect machine can be separated and treated as one production lot. After identifying additional lots obtained from comparable machinery, other subgroups are drawn up and comparisons can be made. Such an approach works well when the investigator needs to isolate a suspected source of variation — for example, improperly functioning machinery or the influence of different operators, different shifts, different input shipments and so on.

The creation of lots from equal quantities of production or from output during equal periods of time requires a different justification. In this case, analysts assume that only common causes of variation are at work. All items in a production lot should therefore be comparable since they are manufactured under equivalent conditions. The practice of defining lots according to equal quantities produced can be used to detect continuous changes in inputs — such as altered chemical solutions. Arrangement according to equal time intervals is an effective way to determine whether the pattern of variation changes over time.

The third method is the simplest. By dispensing with the identification of production lots, investigators are able to select subgroups directly from the manufacturing process. They may choose items produced at regular intervals determined by time or quantity. This practice is popular but has drawbacks. Because production lots are not identified, there is no background information on manufacturing conditions or input characteristics. Regardless of the method chosen, the goal should be to assure that the items in any subgroup have been produced under essentially the same conditions (see Bicking and Gryna, 1974).

## MONITORING PATTERNS OF VARIATION

Once the methods of data collection have been determined and preliminary investigations have been carried out (usually with the help of cause-and-effect charts, Pareto charts and similar tools), analysts are ready to begin monitoring patterns of variation. They do this by constructing *control charts*. These simple but powerful tools serve several purposes. They help the manager to identify different patterns of variation, they enable him to learn more about the underlying causes of variation, and they serve as a framework which can be used to gauge the success of efforts to remove special causes of variation.[5]

Depending on the information sought, different versions of control charts are constructed. All, however, share certain common features. These include a centre line representing the average value for all data collected, and upper and lower control limits which define the boundaries for acceptable levels of variation. The manufacturing process is regarded as being 'in control' if all observations (that is, the averages calculated for each respective subgroup) fall inside the two limits and exhibit no particular trend or tendency. Should any observations lie outside one of the limits — or if a group of observations reveal a distinctive pattern or trend — special causes exist and the process is not in control. Figure 5.7 provides an example of both cases.

The particular type of control chart to be constructed depends on the product characteristics a firm chooses to study. One of the most common applications occurs in the study of 'product attributes'. The term refers to product characteristics that can not be measured on a continuous scale — for example, specifications regarding quality or performance. In order to analyse their product's attributes, managers must first establish 'pass-or-fail' definitions for acceptable levels of quality or performance (see Box 5.4). Once these definitions are in place, engineers can begin to collect data. They will usually be interested in knowing either the number or proportion of items in several subgroups that is defective or otherwise fails to meet acceptable standards.

The actual construction of a control chart to measure product attributes can be illustrated with the help of an example using data taken from an engine assembly plant. After agreeing on pass-or-fail definitions, supervisors and engineers began collecting information on the product's attributes. In this case, 100 engines were inspected for defects each week and it was decided that the weekly results would constitute a 'subgroup'. The inspection process was repeated for 21 successive weeks, meaning that the control chart should have 21 observations or subgroup averages. For each of these weeks, the rejection rate was calculated and the results are reproduced in Figure 5.8. For example, the chart shows that six engines were rejected in the first weekly test of 100, meaning that the rejection rate was 0.06. The central line showing the average

*Figure 5.7    Identifying the causes of variation*

*a) A manufacturing process that is in control*

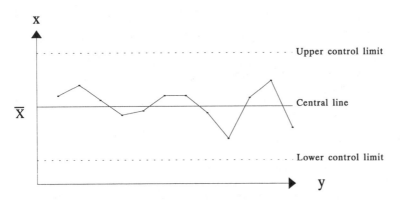

*b) A manufacturing process that is out of control*

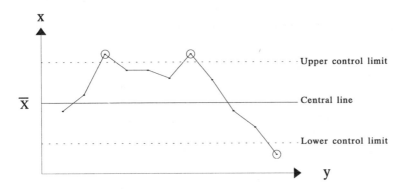

number of defective engines during the entire 21-week test period is 6.24 per 100 inspections. Using these results, engineers can determine the upper and lower control limits which specify the acceptable levels of variation (for formulae and calculations, see the statistical appendix). In our example the upper control limit proves to be 13.5 defectives per 100 inspections. No lower control limit applies, so a practical limit of zero defectives represents the lower boundary.

What does the completed chart tell us? First, the rates of rejection obtained from each weekly inspection range between 0.02 and 0.12. In no week does the proportion of defectives exceed the control limits, meaning that the process of engine assembly is in statistical control. Second, no special causes of variation

---

### Box 5.4   Product attributes and control charts

Many product attributes refer to acceptable levels of performance or quality. The criteria for evaluating these attributes can be expressed in terms of a simple two-way classification: each item either meets, or fails to meet, a pre-determined standard. Examples would be the number of damaged cans in a production lot of a certain size (where the two categories are either 'damaged' or 'undamaged') or the number of items in a subgroup that do not meet specifications. Using these types of definitions, managers can monitor the occurrence of defective items. If the number, or proportion, of defectives is relatively stable over an extended period of time, managers can predict future levels of variation with some confidence.

Not all product attributes can be expressed in terms of pass-or-fail criteria. Slightly different control charts will be used if product attributes are defined by the count of events occurring over time. One version is applicable when attention focuses on characteristics such as the number of surface flaws on a sheet of material, the number of service calls made or the number of customer complaints received. Another is employed if the amount of material or the unit of time for each inspection varies. Relevant examples are: inspection of irregular lengths of woven fabric, the number of blemishes on finished furniture or the number of surface defects in differing lengths of brass strips. For further discussion, see the appendix.

---

exist, so predictions about future performance can be made with some confidence. Rates of defectives, production costs and production schedules can all be forecast with some degree of certainty. Of course, there is no assurance that the assembly process will continue to be stable, or in control, over the longer term. A special source of variation may suddenly emerge. But if it is quickly identified and eliminated, the operation should return to control. Third, if other manufacturing processes in the plant are also in control, managers are in a position to begin improving the entire system and to address the common causes of variation.

In conclusion, the charts and graphs we have described in this chapter are only a part of a larger statistical arsenal which is available to the manager and his employees. Further discussion of SPC is found in the appendix to this book and the manager who hopes to install a system of continuous improvement should begin by consulting that material. It is equally important to bear in mind that the true value of SPC extends far beyond the basic problem-solving examples discussed here. Even bigger returns should be realized as users gain a better picture of the interrelationships between different parts of the production process and begin to collaborate in the search for common and special causes of variation. Finally, the amount of time and energy devoted to SPC will be substantial in the early stages, but this should not be a permanent feature.

*Figure 5.8  Monitoring product attributes: rejection rates in an engine-assembly plant*

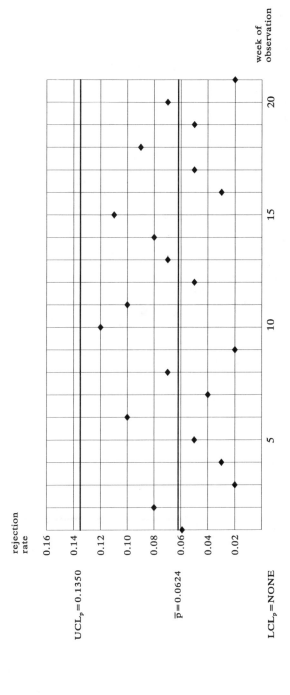

99

Critical parts of the manufacturing system may always require monitoring and control. After a few years, however, the firm should have progressed beyond the basic elements of process control and more of its efforts will be concentrated on other CITs. The following chapter looks at several real-world applications of these tools.

## NOTES

1. For example, workers on a loading dock would want information enabling them to shorten the time and distances travelled by incoming material. Their version of the flow chart would not be as detailed as that provided to engineers who are studying the implementation of cellular work stations along an assembly line.
2. Another, less common approach would be to set up categories reflecting customers' priorities.
3. The appearance of the cause-and-effect chart has led some to call it a 'fishbone chart'. These charts are also known as 'Ishikawa diagrams', after their originator.
4. For further discussion see Kume, 1992, pp. 49–53 or Ishikawa, 1990, pp. 9–14.
5. The removal of special causes, although crucial, does not represent a genuine improvement in the manufacturing process. For example, variation in a product might be caused by the haphazard way tools are arranged and located on an assembly line. Once it is agreed to place the tools in exactly the same way all the time, the variation due to operators fumbling for tools is eliminated. A special cause of variation has been eliminated; when all other special causes are eliminated, the process is in statistical control. Only at this point can the critical work on systemic causes for continuous improvement actually begin.

# 6. Continuous Improvement In Action

The tools and methods discussed in Chapters 4 and 5 are only some of the possibilities available to a CIF. In this chapter we describe in some detail how four firms have used these techniques to achieve substantial gains in quality and productivity. These case studies have been drawn from a larger body of evidence compiled by UNIDO as a by-product of its work to promote continuous improvement in developing countries and transition economies. In many instances, firms have participated in UNIDO-sponsored programmes designed to introduce methods of continuous improvement or to upgrade existing practices. In others, the firms themselves have initiated these programmes with UNIDO staff alongside as observers.

The four manufacturers singled out for discussion here are located in Latin America, Central Europe and Africa. This geographical diversity of firms is deliberate. One of the claims we make in this book is that continuous improvement in manufacturing is not culture-bound. Firms were also chosen to reflect a rather wide range of experience and sophistication in the techniques of continuous improvement. Thus the case studies presented here are meant to show not only how CITs are being used in specific circumstances, but also to demonstrate their generality.

In line with the approach taken in previous chapters, attention focuses on shop-floor experiences even though some of these firms employ methods of continuous improvement in other areas of their operation (for example, involving managerial practices, product design or organizational matters). The first case study deals with the recent experience of the International Division of Packard Electronics. That firm is an experienced user of CITs, which has worked hard to upgrade methods of continuous improvement in one of its larger plants. The second concerns a maker of heavy-duty components for trucks in Central Europe. Because the company had no previous experience with methods of continuous improvement, the technologies it employs are quite different from those found in Packard's plants. An African subsidiary of Matsushita Corporation is the subject of the third case study. It has operated a programme of continuous improvement for a number of years, and is slowly but steadily up-grading these technologies. The chapter concludes with a description of methods employed by Elamex S.A., a large contract manufacturer operating in Mexico and the Caribbean. Like Packard, Elamex is an experienced user of CITs although the principles and methods it relies upon are relevant to manufacturers everywhere.


## PRODUCING ELECTRICAL COMPONENTS IN MEXICO[1]

A multinational with factories in North America, Europe and developing countries, Packard Electric International makes electrical wiring assemblies and related components for automobile and truck manufacturers. Its first plant in Mexico was established in 1978. Today, it operates more than thirty plants located around the country.[2]

An emphasis on product quality and a commitment to continuous improvement have been part of Packard Mexico's approach since its inception. These priorities received an added boost in the mid-1980s when the company was awarded a contract to supply electrical wiring to New United Motor Manufacturing Incorporated (NUMMI), a joint venture of General Motors and Toyota in California. The influence of Toyota's managers and engineers meant that the new car maker was an especially demanding customer.

Immediately after the contract was signed, NUMMI's staff produced a set of quality standards and blueprints containing references that were unknown to engineers and workers in Packard's Mexican plant. The car maker's engineers soon expressed their dissatisfaction with the samples and components being supplied. They also criticized Packard's methods of wrapping the assemblies and rejected several shipments because of variation in the colouring of the cables. Other objections concerned details such as stress marks introduced during assembly.[3] In addition to being a very demanding customer, NUMMI expected Packard Mexico to perform as a JIT supplier. Precise quantities of defect-free products had to be delivered to a customer several hundred miles away. These supplies had to arrive at specified hours of the day, at the correct location in the plant, and at the agreed price.

Managers of the Mexican operation were quick to respond to this challenge. They contacted Sumitomo Wiring, a high quality supplier to Japanese car makers (including Toyota), and arranged that a team of engineers be sent to Mexico for six months. The fact that Packard Mexico was already an experienced practitioner of continuous improvement probably made it easier for the firm to act on the advice from Sumitomo and the suggestions by NUMMI. Existing techniques were quickly upgraded and new, more powerful routines were introduced. The following discussion focuses on some of the more important elements in Packard Mexico's new programme.

**Customer-Focused Production**

The importance of customers' expectations has always been an established part of the manufacturing philosophy of Packard Mexico. However, managers soon realized that with a discriminating buyer like NUMMI, special efforts would be required. They arranged for a resident engineer to work permanently at the customer's California plant, serving as a communications link between NUMMI and Packard Mexico. He maintains daily contact with NUMMI's engineers and operators, monitors the quality of harnesses and other components arriving at the plant and provides instant feedback to his colleagues in Mexico. This arrangement permits Packard to respond promptly to most of NUMMI's problems and encourages a two-way flow of ideas between the firms. For example, Packard's Mexican staff and workers are able to devise process improvements in their own plant that are eventually implemented in the NUMMI plant in California.

**Kanban and Supplier Involvement**

One of Sumitomo's main contributions was to help Packard implement a more effective kanban system. A kanban card showing the code numbers, specifications and production sequence is attached to each item when it enters the factory. The cards remain with the item until it leaves the plant as part of a completed electrical assembly or component. When more material is needed, another kanban card is returned for processing and one or more items are supplied. Cards are also passed to outside suppliers as reorder forms. They serve as a simple form of visual control, pulling material from suppliers and conveying information on the number of pieces ordered, the number built and the number still to be built.

By introducing a more comprehensive system of kanban, Packard Mexico has been able to realize several benefits. Problems of product quality can be quickly traced back to specific manufacturing processes and other opportunities for improvement can be readily identified. For example, the system demonstrated the need for new procedures and rules to be introduced and rigidly followed in order to minimize inventories. Once these methods were in place, Packard was able to cut inventories and related floor space by 80 per cent.

Experience has showed that the effectiveness of kanban is greatly enhanced if customers and suppliers work together closely (see Box 6.1). One of the major objectives of this collaboration is to stabilize the production schedules of each firm. This makes it easier for all collaborators to deliver precise quantities at specified times of the day. Kanban link-ups between suppliers and

**Box 6.1    Involving suppliers in the kanban system**

Suppliers' first reaction to any suggestion that they adopt kanban is usually negative. However, Packard's managers learned that simple and clear requests for cooperation, coupled with assistance in introducing kanban, usually gave positive results. The firm worked hard to demonstrate to suppliers that such a move would be in their own interest as well as in that of Packard.

One challenge came from Packard's own regional warehouse which normally shipped components in very large quantities — often, production lots representing several weeks of inventory. When asked to supply exact amounts at precise times, the warehouse managers argued that they could not divide production lots into smaller quantities without raising prices. Packard's staff met with warehouse personnel to seek a solution to the problem. By employing basic tools of continuous improvement, the team was able to show that the warehouse was also receiving material in undesirably large quantities from its own suppliers. The problem was then discussed with upstream vendors and eventually solved.

In another instance, Packard was able to simplify its unloading procedures significantly. Deliveries had previously been unpredictable. Sometimes long lines of trucks would be waiting to unload, while at other times there were none. Extra employees were kept on duty to handle unpredictable peak periods. With complementary kanban systems, these problems were eliminated. Deliveries arrived on time, all paperwork was prepared beforehand and the material could be promptly unloaded.

customers can also lead to even greater reductions in inventory and other waste. For example, Packard's system requires that smaller quantities of material be shipped in appropriately sized containers. Once the firm was able to convince local suppliers of pallets, boxes and cable of the benefits from kanban, they found this alteration in shipping practices worked to their advantage as well.

**Visual Controls**

Along with its new kanban system, Packard began to rely heavily on visual controls. These effective but inexpensive tools convey important information on problems, procedures and improvements. One example is a large board on the loading dock which shows the time when each set of materials is scheduled to arrive and the supplier providing them. Another is the continuous improvement board (known as *kaizen* to the Japanese). These describe a problem with an accompanying sketch or snapshot of the area to be improved. Underlying causes and corrective actions are noted as well as the team or person responsible for resolving the problem. The expected date for completion of the improvement is shown along with a picture of the desired result.

Other visual controls were used to communicate correct procedures for assembly, maintenance and other operations. First, lines were painted on the floor in storage areas to show where completed products should be placed or where finished cables should be hung so as not to touch the floor. Second, job set-up sheets were posted in front of each cutting machine. Operators refer to these visual instructions if they are unsure about production requirements, job instructions, or methods of packing material for in-process handling. Third, machine down-time was drastically reduced by introducing a Japanese system known as 'andon'. The system consists of green, yellow, and red lights placed over critical equipment. Lights indicate whether the equipment is running properly (green), is temporarily idle (yellow), or is not working and requires attention (red). Andon quickly alerts maintenance and repair personnel to critical equipment problems.

These and other visual controls have become a ubiquitous part of Packard Mexico's operation.[4] They have proven to be a simple low-cost alternative to computer-generated data and a powerful stimulus to improvement. While computer-based systems provide more comprehensive information, the results are often distributed to only a select group of individuals. Recipients may be far removed from the manufacturing process and not understand the impact of such data. There is also likely to be a lag between the time data is collected and when it is made available. As the Packard experience demonstrates, visual controls provide immediate on-site information for all.

**Housekeeping and the Elimination of Waste**

Using standard methods of continuous improvement, Packard had always stressed the need for strict housekeeping practices and the elimination of waste. It was evident, however, that the Japanese advisors' view of waste and housekeeping practices did not coincide with that of their Mexican and American counterparts.[5] During the initial plant audit, the first place the Sumitomo consultants searched was the waste baskets. They were looking for discarded or defective materials, broken or damaged components and similar refuse that could hold important clues to underlying problems.

Employees at Packard's Mexican plants soon recognized that waste included far more than just defective parts or scrap. Inactivity on the part of people or machines, inefficient methods or movements and unnecessary processes (for example, making or passing along a defective unit) were also waste. Excess stock and overproduction was regarded as an expensive miscalculation which tied up money and space and drove up costs. In general, any part of a manufacturing process that does not add value is considered wasteful.

Packard began a search to eliminate waste in every part of its system. An example referring to one particular series of manufacturing steps is found in

Figure 6.1. Each block represents a sequential step with a height proportionate to the time needed to perform that operation. The original sequence required a relatively long amount of processing time and involved three non-value-added steps. Packard's workers began by reorganizing the plant layout. Operators were previously separated from one another by intervening rows of machines. After streamlining, pairs of operators were located back-to-back between rows of facing machines. That arrangement led to a smoother flow of materials, a better exchange of information and enabled managers to match new workers with more experienced operators. With these changes, the firm was able to eliminate one step which added no value and to reduce the amount of processing time significantly.

*Figure 6.1    Packard Mexico's lead-time reduction in one manufacturing process*

*Analysts began by measuring the time required for each step in this manufacturing process. They also determined which steps added value to the product and which did not. The latter, which include operations such as inspection, counting and rework, are shown in shaded boxes. With disciplined effort, Packard was able to eliminate one step and to reduce the time required for most remaining steps.*

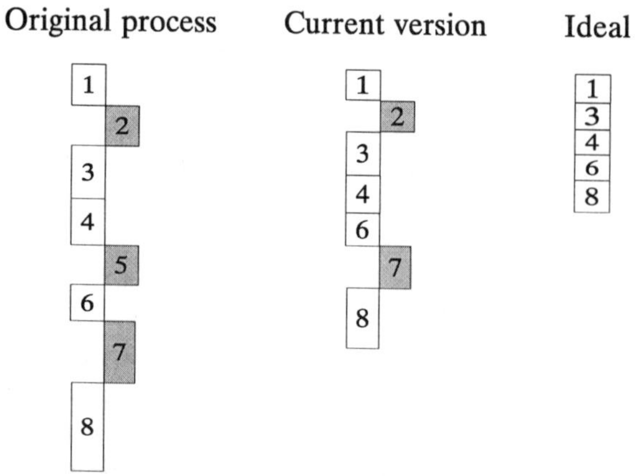

Original process        Current version        Ideal

Source: UNIDO and Packard Electric (International Division, Mexico).

**Planning For Problem Prevention**

Along with their other innovations, managers began to search for ways to prevent problems as well as to correct them. Both approaches cut costs and raise quality, though the former requires more analysis and planning. Teams worked on problem prevention in several different parts of the factory but only improvements on the shop floor are referred to here.

One example relates to a problem which emerged when an improvement team discovered that the number of rejects in a particular manufacturing process was consistently too high. They noted that it was common practice to place all rejected material on large racks. In addition to recommendations designed to reduce the rate of defects, the team suggested that the racks themselves were part of the problem and decided to reduce their size by half. The purpose was to discourage operators from postponing corrective action. Eventually, the racks were removed entirely. That change imposed an even stricter discipline on operators; they were immediately forced to take corrective action whenever a reject was identified.[6]

Teams working in another part of the plant found that they could avoid some forms of waste by altering methods of die-changing for most of the factory's cutting processes. Many of the necessary adjustments are now made on a trial press before the die leaves the crib for the cutter. Because these steps are performed off the production line, problems can be avoided and wasted effort is prevented. As a result, Packard has been able to reduce the time needed for changing dies in its cutting processes by 80 per cent.

Other forms of problem prevention have focused on ways to improve methods of handling and packaging within the plant. One of the more effective techniques was to cover the cement floor around wire harness equipment with thick sections of Astroturf. The new material provides a much softer surface and better cushion, reducing both worker fatigue and product damage. When a terminal falls and is stepped on by an operator, it is harmlessly pushed into Astroturf. Because the solution proved to be so effective, Astroturf is also used to line the bottom of compartments where dies are stored and this, too, prevents expensive damage.

A related modification was to develop protective coverings for the most fragile components. Wiring harnesses are constructed of very fine wire and thin cables which can be easily broken. To prevent damage, workers designed protective coverings for the cable racks. Sensitive parts are wrapped in plastic to prevent contamination that could lead to product failure and special plastic cups are fixed over the ends of wire bundles that are critical to the proper functioning of the product.

Finally, teams noted that components and harnesses were frequently damaged during transport from one part of the factory to another. One reason was the fragile nature of the equipment, but the team also believed the size of the containers was inappropriate. Large containers requiring expensive mechanical transport had been the favoured method of moving materials inside the plant. The solution was to use small containers that could be easily carried by one person. The adjustment not only allowed workers to exercise more care about in-plant transport but also eliminated expensive material-handling machinery and helped to reduce inventories of work-in-process.

## Worker Training

To support its programme of continuous improvement, Packard operates an elaborate programme of employee training. Every new operator begins with forty hours of classroom training, forty hours of product orientation and forty hours of work alongside a trained operator. All operators receive multi-station training, with each worker learning the routines for his own station as well as that of the preceding station and the following one. This approach emphasizes the fact that each person on the production line is both a customer and a supplier and improves the flow of site-specific information.

Training in all of Packard Electric's Mexican plants has been intensified following the NUMMI contract. The extended programme, which is summarized in Figure 6.2, stresses customer relations, control over variation and continuous improvement. Training is in a series of modules, with all employees receiving thorough instruction in basic areas such as the meaning and importance of process variation, the use of improvement tools and the need for teamwork. Team members are taught how to collect and interpret basic kinds of data, while team leaders and selected operators are given instruction in SPC, data collection and display and the use of various graphs and charts. Instructors emphasize the need to exploit on-site production information. A great deal of time is spent explaining the importance and meaning of various tracking measures. All trainees understand that such information is designed to aid improvement efforts rather than compare or punish workers.

An even more ambitious approach is the creation of multidisciplinary teams which are trained to apply Packard's five-step process to solving problems (see Box 6.2). These teams are formed to investigate areas of the plant that are most in need of improvement. Engineers, operators, and supervisors collaborate on proposed solutions which stress quick results. When their plan is ready, the part of the plant that is the subject of analysis is shut down. Machines may be ripped from the floor, walls removed, workstations relocated and transport lines altered. All this is accomplished in only a few days. Operators working in this section of the plant are part of the effort and will clearly understand their new role when the changes are complete. When production resumes, data is collected and posted so that all can see the increased performance.[7]

*Figure 6.2* *Modular training in Packard's Mexican plants*

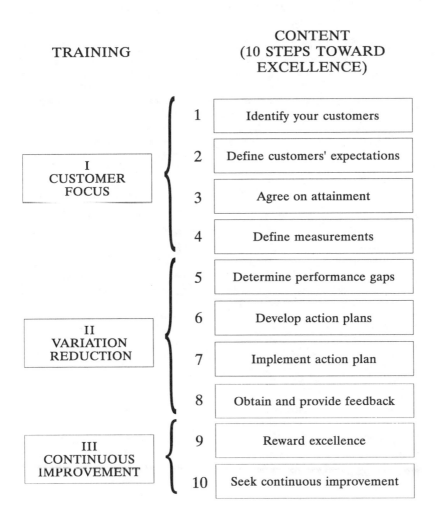

TRAINING

CONTENT
(10 STEPS TOWARD
EXCELLENCE)

| I CUSTOMER FOCUS |  | |
|---|---|---|
|  | 1 | Identify your customers |
|  | 2 | Define customers' expectations |
|  | 3 | Agree on attainment |
|  | 4 | Define measurements |

II VARIATION REDUCTION

| | 5 | Determine performance gaps |
| | 6 | Develop action plans |
| | 7 | Implement action plan |
| | 8 | Obtain and provide feedback |

III CONTINUOUS IMPROVEMENT

| | 9 | Reward excellence |
| | 10 | Seek continuous improvement |

*Source*: Packard Electric International.

**Box 6.2    Packard's five-step process to solving problems**

Packard uses teams made up of operators and supervisors from various parts of the plant to investigate and solve problems. When a problem is isolated, its 'natural owners' (usually, those responsible for that part of the manufacturing process immediately prior to detection) are identified. For example, operators who pass damaged material to the next step in an assembly process are the natural owner. This designation assigns no blame. Instead, the natural owner becomes responsible for coordinating the search for solutions. The search proceeds according to the following five steps.

1. **Identify and define the problem.** The scope of the problem should be clear to the entire team. All members should be able to contribute to the work.

2. **Take immediate action.** The group should take immediate action to prevent any repetition of the problem. Steps may involve product containment, sorting or recall to 'clean' all the stock between the supplier and the customer. Steps 1 and 2 should be done in two days.

3. **Root-cause analysis.** All possible reasons for the difficulty should be analysed to determine the probable contribution of each to the problem. The natural owner can then be confirmed and involved as a team member. This person could be different from the owner originally identified when the problem was discovered. Step 3 should take a maximum of 10 days.

4. **Irreversible corrective action and follow-up.** Once the causes are identified, corrective action must be taken. Product and process conditions will be monitored to ensure that the corrective action shows good results. If Step 4 takes more than 30 days, the customer must be informed of progress.

5. **Verification.** The situation is monitored until it is clear that the problem is solved. Customer reports indicating zero defects are the usual means of monitoring. This procedure is not begun until the manufacturing process has stabilized following the corrective action taken in Step 4. The verification period is usually from 30 to 90 days.

*Source*: Packard Electric International.

Although the technique can be very effective, not all processes are amenable to quick improvement. Many will only yield to steady incremental efforts and some may be impervious to such efforts. Nevertheless, Packard's programme of training and group improvement has paid back the costs of training many times over. Managers also noted that the method boosted morale since team members could see the immediate result of their own efforts. Significantly, all these gains were achieved not by shedding labour or increasing the operators' workload, but rather through the reorganization of the plant.

In conclusion, the firm's emphasis on continuous improvement has yielded impressive results. In the first year of its contract with NUMMI, Packard's Mexican plant received 102 reports of quality problems. By the second year the number had dropped to 47, and in the third year — when NUMMI installed 2.7 million car harnesses — the Packard plant received only 10 reports of quality problems. The firm's success in reducing waste was no less impressive. When it began to supply NUMMI, its weekly reports showed overproduction of up to 22 per cent for some parts and underproduction of 12 per cent for others. Three years later, weekly production levels varied by only 0.001 per cent. Production reports were eventually discontinued because improvement efforts had made them superfluous. Packard's other plants report similar successes thanks to a disciplined approach to continuous improvement.

# MAKING TRUCK COMPONENTS IN CENTRAL EUROPE

The firm providing the information for this study is a Hungarian producer of truck components which embarked on a UNIDO-assisted programme of continuous improvement in 1991. One of these components, a hydraulic clutch controller for use in heavy-duty trucks and buses, is the focus of discussion here. This study focuses on a modest, but important, first step in the improvement process.

Managers of this plant were keenly aware that several areas of their operation were in need of improvement. Conditions in the plant were characterized by disorder and an uneven flow of work which contributed to waste and a build-up of inventory, work-in-process and finished goods. This confusion was compounded by a managerial tendency to address isolated problems (for example, by constantly shifting operators from one assembly line to another) without developing a more systematic plan for improvement. One result of these practices was an unacceptably high rate of defects — 13 per cent in the case of clutch controllers.

Managers' first response was to form several teams to study every facet of the assembly process. The controller itself is assembled from seven pieces, namely, a pedal, housing, rim, cover plate, assisting piston, hydraulic piston, and double valve. Team members were recruited from every part of the operation and received special training before beginning the improvement programme. Employees were informed of the new drive for improvement and assured that no one would lose their job as a result of productivity improvements. Managers also pledged their full support to the project and granted teams the authority to enact sweeping recommendations and make experimental changes.

Among the instructions the improvement teams received, the following were especially noteworthy:

- **Adopt measurable goals and depend only on measurable results**. A heavy emphasis was placed on validation of the team's recommendations. The requirement that goals and results be measurable forced the teams to be realistic about their assessments and recommendations.

- **Teams should exhibit a bias in favour of action.** The goal was to take action on many fronts and demonstrate results quickly. Preference was given to identification of small improvements rather than costly, large-scale remedies requiring new technologies.

- **Not all solutions can be thoroughly tested, much less implemented, in the current phase.** Follow-up work will be essential to implement suggestions and recommendations which are medium term in duration.

With this background, each team began to gather information on different parts of the assembly system. It was soon agreed that all operations could be logically divided into two easily distinguishable subsystems. The first was carried out at four individual workstations where the hydraulic piston, the rim, the cover plate and the pedal were fitted together.[8] The second was the final assembly of the controller itself. The latter set of operations were performed at six workstations and the following description focuses exclusively on that subsystem.

Analysis began with the construction of flow charts documenting the operations at each workstation. Every step performed at a workstation was carefully studied and any unnecessary movements were noted. Examples included: picking up a part with the right hand from the left side of the workstation; transferring parts from one hand to the other; the practice of removing parts (washers, screws, bolts or nuts) from storage boxes and spreading them over the worktable; and the need to separate different parts which had accidentally or erroneously been stored together. Details such as these were used later to improve operating procedures. Figure 6.3 provides an example, showing the flow chart for workstation 1, where the housing is fitted with the cover plate.

Another team gathered data on the operating times at each workstation. These were recorded repeatedly and the averages are reported in Table 6.1; the operating times and capacities of each workstation vary greatly. Such imbal-

*Figure 6.3    Flow chart for assembly of the housing and cover plate*

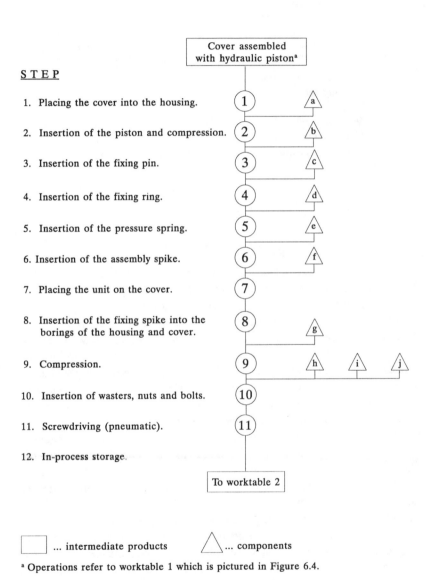

S T E P

1.  Placing the cover into the housing.

2.  Insertion of the piston and compression.

3.  Insertion of the fixing pin.

4.  Insertion of the fixing ring.

5.  Insertion of the pressure spring.

6.  Insertion of the assembly spike.

7.  Placing the unit on the cover.

8.  Insertion of the fixing spike into the
    borings of the housing and cover.

9.  Compression.

10.  Insertion of wasters, nuts and bolts.

11.  Screwdriving (pneumatic).

12.  In-process storage.

... intermediate products        ... components

[a] Operations refer to worktable 1 which is pictured in Figure 6.4.

*Table 6.1    Current operation times of final assembly process*

| Work-station | Operation | Times (in seconds) | Capacity (per shift) |
|---|---|---|---|
| 1 | Housing and cover plate | 75.7 | 323 |
| 2 | Housing and rim | 46.2 | 530 |
| 3 | Pedal | 47.2 | 519 |
| 4 | Valve-gap adjuster | 43.7 | 560 |
| 5 | Inspection test | 114.7 | 213 |
| 6 | Finishing operation | 58.5 | 418 |
| | **Total** | **386.0** | |

*Source*: UNIDO.

ances are one reason for the accumulation of inventories and the uneven load on operators. It is clear that the major bottleneck occurs at workstation 5. The relatively large amount of time required to complete inspection tests and the limited capacity at this workstation disrupt the flow of work.

Improvement teams also studied the planned flow of materials during the final assembly process. Inputs and parts from central stores were kept on shelves next to the assembly line where they were needed. Parts for the workstations were mainly stored in boxes on pallets located directly behind the operators. The group noted that parts were kept in several different kinds of storage containers (Bosch-type wooden cases, standardized boxes with organized compartments and polyethylene and paper bags).

Finally, a team examined the layout of the process which is replicated in Figure 6.4. Sub-assembly workstations are shown for completeness, although the description here focuses mainly on the final assembly. A large inventory of goods-in-process was needed between workstations 1 and 2 in order to buffer the capacity differences between the two sets of operations. The capacities at workstations 2, 3 and 4 were more closely aligned and required no similar buffers. However, a build-up of goods-in-process occurred both before and after operations at workstation 5. This phase of the assembly process required the longest period of time; throughput capacity at this point was less than half that of the preceding and following operations.

Recommendations which emerged from the exercise fall into three categories. One set consists of those proposals which were rejected, usually because they required significant additional investments and therefore violated the

*Figure 6.4 Original layout of assembly area for clutch controllers*

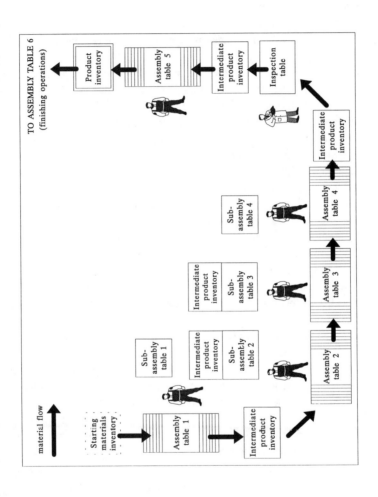

teams' original mandate.[9] A second set is recommendations which require a longer period of time for testing and implementation. Finally, there were several proposals that entailed small changes in procedures; these could be tested and implemented during the time allotted to the investigation. The last two sets of recommendations are discussed below.

Proposals which were immediately tested and became part of standard procedures involved changes in operators' practices and alterations in the layout of the assembly line and the work cell. The 5-S exercise (described in Chapter 4) proved a very effective means to identify some of these improvements. One result was to move the entire assembly line 60 centimetres away from the wall to permit cleaning of the shop floor and to allow easy access to all machines for maintenance. Shelf space was designated to store the inventories needed at each particular stage in the assembly line. It was agreed that each component and part would be stored in a specific place with the method of storage indicated next to the name and code number of that piece. All unnecessary objects were removed from the in-plant transport routes. A parking area was also set aside for the transport vehicles used on the assembly line. Under the new procedures each vehicle should be returned to its designated space immediately after use. Finally, the assembly line was redesigned in a U-shaped configuration. This change reduced the distance materials travelled between workstations.

Changes in operators' procedures included an agreement that tool boards be placed at the backside of the worktable. The most frequently used tools would now be positioned closest to the operator. The location of parts and components was altered so that they were in easy reach and better conformed with the work sequence. Sufficient quantities should always be available for one shift with special in-plant transportation to ensure the supply of some components. Tests showed that the new arrangements significantly reduced operating times.

Two additional improvements were made in the design and construction of the clutch controller. First, a review of the product design and engineering documents revealed that the position of the pedal was determined by use of screws and bolts of several different sizes. Neither function nor space constraints justified these differences and it was agreed that the dimensions of these materials would be standardized. Second, the current assembly process included several drilling operations. Some of these steps could be eliminated by designing rivets into the cast-iron housing. This adaptation saved time and avoided defects due to inaccurate drilling.

The net effect of all these improvements was to cut the number of sub-assembly stations from four to two. Some of the remaining sub-assembly operations were combined, while others were moved to the final assembly line in order to smooth out the flow of production material. Floor space was also reduced because of the new assembly layout and smaller amount of storage space that was required for inventories.

Among the proposals requiring more time to test and implement, the most important dealt with problems of quality. One team carefully examined each defective controller to determine the source of the defects. Altogether, ten different types of defects were identified. Each one, along with the frequency of its occurrence, is noted in Figure 6.5. The three most common defects are

*Figure 6.5  Pareto diagram of product defects, by category*

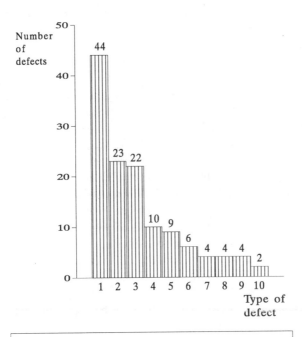

Type of defect:

1. Air escapes when the pedal is applied.
2. Air escapes under normal conditions.
3. Oil escapes between the housing and the pedal.
4. Movement of the pedal is impeded.
5. Controller reacts slowly to the application of the pedal.
6. Controller functions by intermittent movements.
7. Air escapes during pressure test.
8. Leaking between the rim and the piston.
9. Piston is cracked.
10. Operating pressure is lower than required.

that air escapes, either when the pedal is applied or is at rest, and that oil escapes from the housing and pedal. About 70 per cent of all defects can be attributed to one of these causes. This initial exercise yielded numerous incremental benefits based on the use of shared information and effective analytical tools. Management completely support this drive to improve. A first step such as this demonstrates to managers and team members that significant improvements can be made without costly or sophisticated machinery.


## HOUSEHOLD ELECTRONICS IN EAST AFRICA[10]

In operation for almost 30 years, the firm described here is a subsidiary of Matsushita, one of Japan's largest multinationals. The parent company and the local firm share the same emphasis on continuous improvement, production standards and company strategies. In other ways, the subsidiary enjoys a large measure of independence. Of the 450 people it employs, only four are expatriates.[11] The head office supplies high-level training and technology (for which it is paid royalties), but rarely provides financial support. The subsidiary is expected to surmount any financial difficulties by becoming more efficient.

Local production began with batteries and gradually expanded to include portable radios, radio cassette recorders and gramophones. A prolonged economic slump during the 1980s forced the company to scale back its operation. Monthly production in 1992 was 4.5 million batteries and around 10,000 radios and cassette recorders. With this level of production, turnover is $11–12 million per year. These figures are only a third of the levels recorded during the late 1970s, yet the operation remains profitable.

Despite sluggish economic conditions and aggressive competition from cheap East Asian imports, this firm has maintained leadership in all its product markets. Much of this success can be explained by the firm's emphasis on quality control and continuous improvement. Various technologies and techniques are in place at every stage of production, from the arrival of inputs to packaging. Quality assurance groups are constantly active on the production line, with hourly and daily samples being tested in the quality control laboratory. These controls, coupled with the high standards which the parent company sets for inputs, have meant that defective products are rare (0.2 per cent for radios and 0.02 per cent for batteries).

The subsidiary's programme of continuous improvement is a comprehensive one and only selected features are discussed here. One of these, worker training, is essential for any CIF, but assumes even greater significance in view of local conditions. The quality of the local workforce was discussed at length during a series of UNIDO-sponsored workshops in East Africa which were attended by 80 firms — including the managers of this Matsushita subsidiary (see UNIDO, 1991). Participants argued that there are serious flaws in existing programmes for tertiary training. The available courses do not prepare graduates to meet changing professional demands, nor provide them with the ability to assimilate imported technologies. A number of management courses are available, but there are none for industrial management.

The effects of poor training are compounded by circumstances which have hindered individuals' abilities to engage in independent decision-making. State-run enterprises have been dominant in the manufacturing sector and are characterized by a top-down command structure which is usually headed by a political appointee rather than a businessman. This has resulted in a critical shortage of managers who can make decisions independently or engage in constructive teamwork.

Because of these circumstances, the firm employs unique and stringent recruitment policies.[12] Applicants for technical jobs must have vocational training and those for middle management must have completed secondary school. All new employees are young — seldom over 23 years of age. This practice reflects managers' opinion that younger workers are more open to new methods and better able to adapt to the company's manufacturing philosophy. The same line of reasoning excludes all university graduates. Though a few have applied for jobs, many do not see themselves as 'workers' and none have been hired. The head of personnel argues that such formal qualifications reduce the willingness to learn new techniques and make it difficult to accept the company's 'family atmosphere'.

The subsidiary could not enforce these criteria without having its own capability to educate new recruits. All new employees receive up to 12 months of (paid) on-the-job training. Japanese instructors were originally used, but now training is done by locals employed in the factory. Foremen receive an additional year of full-time training at a local vocational centre or at the government-run centre for high technology which was originally established with the firm's assistance. When managers are recruited from secondary school, they are assigned to work on a production line for several months to get acquainted with actual working conditions. This unusual procedure encounters some resistance, but those who have been through the experience report that they have become better managers as a result.

Despite all this training, many new managers remain sceptical of the company's policies and organizational methods and some even regard them as incomprehensible. To resolve this problem, all managers are sent to the parent company's foreign training institute in Japan after a period of service. There they receive full-scale training in a programme developed by Matsushita. First-hand observation of the working environment and company culture greatly improved each trainee's understanding of the overall approach. According to the subsidiary's managing director, this experience is even more important than the actual skills acquired.

Training programmes concern not just the technical details of the job, but also tools of continuous improvement and company philosophy. Included are various aspects of statistical process control, the 5-S routine, practices to encourage workers to share information and other methods. The importance of these methods is reinforced by visual aids scattered around the factory. Refresher courses, in-house training sessions and evening classes cover matters like cost reduction and standardization. Promotion within the company is not possible without satisfactorily completing these courses.

A second pillar of the company's continuous improvement programme is its maintenance system. All machinery is Japanese in origin, most of it dating back to the 1960s. The more complicated spare parts are imported from Japan, but all alterations in the plant layout and improvements in machinery and equipment are carried out by local staff. Some of this work is done by specialized maintenance units, though every employee is actively involved in the maintenance system. Operators are expected to keep their machinery clean and in good working order. Plant managers exercise supervisory control, while the specialized maintenance teams carry out daily inspections. Major overhauls and general cleaning operations take place during long holidays.

The fact that the company remains highly competitive while using equipment that is up to 25 years old attests to the effectiveness of its maintenance system. Other indicators confirm this impression. Labour productivity, for example, is higher than at any time in the firm's history, and reportedly matches that of Matsushita subsidiaries in other parts of the world. Meanwhile, the overall rate of capacity utilization is around 90 per cent. This figure far exceeds that of other manufacturers. With daily power cuts and policy restrictions on imports (owing to a shortage of foreign exchange), the average rate of capacity utilization in neighbouring factories is only 20 to 25 per cent.

There are plans to upgrade the maintenance system before purchasing new equipment and machinery.[13] A new training programme was introduced in 1993 which will eventually lead to a system of total productive maintenance (TPM). The new system is a comprehensive approach to production management which aims at 'zero defects, zero down time, zero accidents and zero absenteeism'. With courses spread over three years, the programme provides training in TPM to staff at all levels. Managers are confident that such an ambitious version of TPM is feasible.

Another noteworthy feature of the firm's continuous improvement programme is its emphasis on policy deployment, an approach described in Chapter 4. Overall objectives are set out by management in the yearly business plan. The Managing Director and Divisional Heads meet daily to discuss current issues and resolve problems. Workers also regularly discuss production problems with foremen and supervisors. All of these meetings pay particular attention to costs. Information on production costs is kept up to date and prominently displayed around the plant. So, too, are examples of cost savings, along with clear explanations of how these savings were accomplished. A rigorous system of internal auditing means that financial performance is carefully monitored and that actual production costs are constantly checked against targets.

In addition to cost control, these procedures are intended to make the management process clear to workers. A cornerstone of the firm's philosophy is that managers' decisions and actions must be understood by employees if their contribution to the firm is to be maximized. While the involvement of workers should not be overrated, it has resulted in a number of improvements. Examples include the modification of a radio model to reduce the occurrence of short circuits, time and paper savings through simplified administrative routines, better plant layout and compensation for power cuts by working overtime.

A final noteworthy feature concerns Matsushita's links with distributors and suppliers. It operates a network of agents and service centres throughout the region. All receive regular visits from a company representative and report back to the firm every month, supplying information on consumer complaints, servicing problems and related matters. Matsushita helps these firms to incorporate elements of continuous improvement and total quality control into their own operations. The subsidiary also provides assistance in production management and consumer services. The main purpose of all this assistance is to improve the quality of goods supplied and ensure that items are delivered on schedule.

In conclusion, the success of this East African manufacturer is largely due to its mastery of certain techniques of continuous improvement. Though the firm has not fully achieved its declared goal of converting employees into 'co-managers', they are the source of many useful ideas and are highly motivated. Such results offer convincing testimony that continuous improvement can be an effective option even in the most difficult economic settings.

## CONTRACT MANUFACTURING IN THE CARIBBEAN AND MEXICO[14]

Elamex S.A. is the ninth largest contract manufacturer in North America and its operations have grown extensively over the last decade. One reason for this growth is that many manufacturers of complex products no longer make all the components and parts they require. Instead, they engage other firms to provide some of these items through a practice known as 'out-sourcing' (see Box 6.3). Elamex works on a contractual basis, assembling and manufacturing components and other items required by its customers. It provides the plant facilities, labour, engineering and management expertise and any equipment that may be needed in these operations.

With considerable experience with methods of continuous improvement, Elamex is capable of providing JIT deliveries throughout North America.[15] Among its customers are some of the world's largest and most sophisticated corporations. Clients include makers of automobiles, computers, aircraft and photographic equipment as well as suppliers of complex products such as information systems and aerospace systems. Its diverse experience with

---

**Box 6.3    Out-sourcing and global competition**

Many firms have found that their costs can be reduced if the job of assembling or making some parts and items is subcontracted out to other manufacturers. Frequently known as out-sourcing, this practice has accelerated the transfer of manufacturing activities from industrialized to developing countries. There are many reasons for its popularity. Suppliers in developing countries may have access to cheap labour and enjoy a competitive advantage in labour-intensive products. Other factors may be strategic location, extremely favourable rates of taxation and national regulations requiring that a certain proportion of a product's final value be added in the country where the product is sold.

Critics argue that out-sourcing rarely yields a significant transfer of skills and technologies, and that profits tend to be repatriated rather than reinvested. Some believe that the method generates little investment or few linkages with other parts of the host economy. They also regard out-sourcing operations as 'footloose', meaning that plants can be quickly relocated if inflation or other circumstances should erode a country's cost advantage.

Whatever the validity of these charges, we believe that the relationship between manufacturing customers and their out-sourcing partners is changing for two reasons. First, price is no longer the sole criterion for competitive success; quality, reliability and timeliness are other important attributes which the supplier must now satisfy. Second, many of the firms that have created these out-sourcing networks have themselves moved from an inspection-bound system of mass production to one relying on continuous improvement and total quality control. Their suppliers must provide JIT delivery, maintain strict process controls and demonstrate flexible shop-floor procedures that coincide with those of the buyers. The maker of the finished product or parent firm is usually willing to supply the necessary technical and financial assistance. These relationships are changing the nature of out-sourcing. The supplier is no longer a passive participant whose only contribution to the finished product is through the cheap labour it employs. Out-sourcing is increasingly becoming a partnership in production. As it does, the opportunities for learning and diffusion of continuous improvement and other technologies grow.

different products, customers and industries, coupled with its emphasis on continuous improvement, makes it an ideal subject for closer study.

A sophisticated firm such as this one employs a wide range of techniques and a simple account of specific applications can not adequately describe the central role of continuous improvement. Instead, some of the major features of the firm's approach are discussed and supplemented with selected examples. Two of the most important of these features concern the firm's methods of controlling work-in-process (WIP) and its concepts of manufacturing lead time.

**Understanding the Significance of Work-in-Process**

Control over WIP is a central goal of Elamex's programme of continuous improvement. This emphasis stems from the fact that WIP is the only part of a manufacturing system where value can be added by the producer.

Though obvious, this point is ignored by a majority of contract manufacturers in developing countries. Cost overruns, process control problems and scheduling lapses are common, suggesting that most of these companies have little control over their WIP. The sources of difficulty are all too evident. Floor space is consumed by racks and pallets of materials and partly finished items while operators wait for critical shortages to be filled. Unnecessarily large teams of workers, engineers and even supervisors are employed just to move materials around the factory. Meanwhile, shoddy maintenance and a shortage of parts means that machinery does not function properly and can not be repaired. In situations such as these, the firm has lost control over WIP and its indirect and direct costs are unnecessarily high.

Elamex's own efforts to control WIP make use of several techniques. Three important techniques are:

- a heavy emphasis on visual controls;

- creation of focused manufacturing centres;

- early implementation of an overall plan for improvement.

Visual controls were perfected in Japan's automobile assembly plants, but the practice has spread to many other industries and is employed throughout the world. Elamex uses it extensively in Mexico where it assembles electronic and electromechanical components and in affiliated operations in the Dominican Republic and Costa Rica. The system's major advantage is to ensure that the occurrence of any abnormal operating conditions will be immediately recognized. To function properly, each work area must be arranged so that the flow of work through the area can be visually managed.

Alternative methods of controlling the work flow are: (i) tracking and reporting procedures which are managed from a site outside the work area; and (ii) methods of performance planning that make use of historical standards as a basis for scheduling operations. Visual controls have proven to be superior to both. They are faster, simpler and cheaper than a computerized system for tracking and reporting and provide more comprehensive information than a set of historical standards based on performance and work measurement. The latter types of indicators tell us very little about the overheads associated with WIP (for example, the costs of handling materials and parts, inventory storage, preparation of tools, job set-up or equipment down-time). In general, Elamex's long experience has convinced the firm that visible controls are an effective management procedure for achieving high-quality results from labour-intensive operations.

A second part of the firm's programme to control WIP is the creation of focused manufacturing centres (FMCs). An entire factory can be organized along these lines, though more often the method is applied to a dedicated production line or manufacturing process. Whatever the application, each FMC is designed to function as a self-contained cost centre and focuses on a particular set of operations.

An FMC is made up of one or more cells, each of which consists of a small group of multiskilled operators and a supervisor. Together, this group will have the authority and responsibility to expedite throughput of WIP. A typical cell includes six or seven assembly operators and a supervisor who determines the rate of WIP throughput and functions as test technician, group leader and planner. Members of the cell are responsible for managing all materials as well as testing, inspection, packaging and related documentation. Cells are closely linked with their suppliers and customers in other parts of the manufacturing system. For example, the last step in a work sequence (usually testing) serves as a 'pull-signal' for suppliers at the preceding stage in the production system.

Elamex analysts have a rather specific set of options to work through before they recommend the creation of an FMC. The cheapest way of creating these cells is by rearranging the shop floor and this is always the preferred alternative. If tooling changes are also required, the costs of conversion to FMC are higher and analysts must be convinced that the benefits will also be greater. The most expensive option would involve new capital investments as well as tooling changes and shop-floor adjustments. That possibility would be considered only if other options are not practical.[16]

Significantly, neither FMCs nor visual controls will be effective unless they are part of an overall plan for improvement. Operations can not be simplified and wasteful procedures eliminated until each process cost has been carefully analysed. Such an approach represents a fundamental departure from more traditional methods where cost reductions are achieved by shedding indirect personnel without altering production processes and methods. Nor is it sufficient to develop improvement plans which apply to one or a few divisions in the factory. That approach merely shifts problems to other types of operations and creates greater inefficiencies elsewhere in the production system (see Box 6.4).

## Manufacturing Lead Times

Elamex's emphasis on WIP is reinforced by its efforts to reduce 'manufacturing lead time'. The term refers to the total amount of time required to make a product and is measured from the time when materials enter the plant until they are shipped out as finished goods. Analysts identify five operations during processing on the shop floor that add to manufacturing lead time. These are known as set-up, run, wait, move and queue.

---

**Box 6.4    Coordinating improvement efforts**

The first place where traditional manufacturing firms try to cut costs is the payroll for indirect personnel such as production supervisors, maintenance personnel, inspectors or production control staff. They can boost profits in the short term by reducing this component of their workforce. But without accompanying improvements in production processes, the gains tend to be short-lived. Performance eventually suffers and costs rise since the services needed to support the present form of production operations are no longer available.

This short-sightedness can be rectified if the firm develops an improvement plan. It will be of little benefit if the plan considers only part of the production system. That approach is self-defeating because it again creates bottlenecks or adds to existing inefficiencies in upstream or downstream operations. This danger can be illustrated from the experience of Elamex staff who were asked to advise a customer on ways to eliminate a bottleneck in a specific production process. They recommend the creation of a series of small production cells similar to the FMCs described here. The change accelerated throughput, eliminated certain steps which added no value and raised quality. However, by insisting that one sick production process be treated in isolation, the customer merely transferred its problems to other parts of the production system. In this case the bottleneck shifted upstream to the raw materials warehouse. Further analysis revealed the need for additional material handlers. When these workers were added, the bottleneck was transferred to the final assembly and testing phase. Once these problems were resolved, all processing areas were coordinated and shipments increased by 67 per cent over the next 12 months. The danger is that without a comprehensive improvement plan, many firms fail to see the interlinkages between different parts of their production system and give up their efforts long before realizing any results.

Set-up represents the time spent preparing workstations to accept or process incoming materials. It includes changeover time in the case of downstream operations. The amount of time required for these preparatory operations depends on the job sequence and the steps included in each manufacturing process. Because the form, fit or function of a workpiece is not altered, set-up is an indirect labour activity or form of waste that should always be targeted for reduction. Engineers strive to reduce set-up times in three ways:

- Tooling and tool changeovers can be simplified so that set-ups can take place concurrently with production of other parts. Quick set-ups and changeovers can be planned and executed on conveyor lines, presses, moulding machines and other machinery if the manufacturing process is understood and thoroughly analysed. Simplification is always the first option as it requires little if any tooling or capital expense.

- Engineers can reduce the time required for changeovers by redesigning a manufacturing process, developing new forms of tool design and tool handling and altering plant layout and control procedures. Using these principles, Elamex has cut the time for retooling and changeovers to less than 10 minutes on several production lines.

- Careful planning of production and an optimal sequence of operations can further reduce set-up times. Sometimes known as 'finite scheduling', this requires that specific types of information be available immediately as events occur. Examples include a count of production pieces, process yields and machinery availability (including down-time and scheduled maintenance periods). Such data can be collected inexpensively by systems of cards, flags or lights. More advanced reporting systems make use of computer-aided planning tools.

The second component of manufacturing lead time is the 'run time' and is the only part of the entire sequence when value is being added to the product. Direct costs are incurred during this period of time as the form, fit or function of a workpiece is altered by manual labour, machinery or some other processing apparatus. For planners and engineers working on these operations, the ultimate goal is the continuous flow of material — with no stoppages and the elimination of all non-value-added activities. Run time is fixed once the processing method has been selected and any reduction will usually involve additional spending for new capital equipment.

The third and fourth contributors to manufacturing lead time occur when materials are waiting to be used or are being moved around the factory. Both operations represent indirect costs and are obvious targets for improvement efforts. Waiting time can be reduced by avoiding long production runs and striking a proper balance between the various production-line operations.[17] In the case of moving time, the ideal situation is for incoming material to be placed at the first work centre immediately after unloading and then follow an uninterrupted passage through the production process. Any cutbacks in moving time will not only reduce manufacturing lead time, but can also lead to savings on in-plant equipment for transport. Elamex, for example, has managed to reduce its spending for cranes, conveyors and other types of material-handling devices. Both waiting and moving time can be cut through improvements in procedures for handling materials and alterations in the factory layout.

Queuing is the last component in total processing time. Another indirect cost, queuing can be reduced through improved management of materials and production processes. When process planning is poor or the process is unstable, the time and costs associated with queuing rises. Queuing practices are generally established by company policies and must be continually reviewed, since any inefficiencies that are inadvertently introduced could become an accepted part of a company's overall resource plan.

An analysis of manufacturing lead time can yield valuable insights about a plant's operations (see Box 6.5). If large amounts of lead time are absorbed by waiting, moving and queuing, this is a strong indication of poor planning, sloppy scheduling and inadequate information flows. The probability of defects also rises if the amount of time materials spend waiting, being moved around the plant or queuing is allowed to increase. Defects logically require that more time be devoted to wasteful operations which add no value and lead to higher indirect costs.

**Responding to Change with Continuous Improvement**

Elamex's efforts to control WIP and reduce manufacturing lead times are central features of the firm's overall strategy. In this section we examine how one of the firm's plants employed these concepts to improve its competitive position.

The Elamex factory described here works on a contractual basis, supplying precision assemblies to makers of computer equipment. The quality of these assemblies had been satisfactory, although other performance indicators were less impressive. The plant's record for on-time delivery was poor and its production costs were relatively high. Neither of these problems had received much attention until an abrupt change in the business climate forced managers to reassess their situation. While the plant had typically carried six months of

---

**Box 6.5   Manufacturing lead time and control of work-in-process**

It is not unusual for analysts to find that the manufacturing lead time in a particular plant is expressed in weeks or months, even though the actual run time can be measured in minutes or hours. In one instance, Elamex engineers working with a large customer found that a typical manufactured part remained in WIP for four to six months, although the standard run time was around 60 hours (less than 2 per cent of the manufacturing lead time).

In a second example, Elamex was asked to analyse the cost structure of a customer producing blades for turbine engines. Investigators were surprised to find that indirect and overhead costs accounted for 68 per cent of total production costs. The high proportion was explained by the fact that, on average, materials were in WIP for 89 days, although the actual run time was only 17 minutes. The big disparity was due to poor scheduling, erratic work flow, a lack of process control, limited information on operations and a large number of unplanned process changeovers. Among the other costs incurred by this firm, 'quality costs' (caused by lack of formal tolerance control and poor monitoring of manufacturing processes) were a quarter of the total, while labour accounted for only 7 per cent.

---

orders, its order book unexpectedly dwindled to less than six weeks of work. The significance of this decline was accentuated by other factors. Several of the plant's customers were retooling before introducing new product lines. Others were retrenching and had decided to cut back on the number of the suppliers. All these customers were pressing their suppliers to meet new, more stringent standards. If Elamex's plant wished to retain its market, it would have to reduce prices, improve the quality of its products and begin JIT deliveries.

Plant managers reacted immediately by agreeing on a new set of goals to meet customers' demands. They included cost reductions, defect-free assemblies and JIT delivery. Once these objectives were endorsed by key personnel, an improvement plan was drawn up and carefully explained to all employees. A vigourous in-house programme of retraining was then launched. Meanwhile, various teams were organized to implement the improvement plan, identify ways of simplifying production processes and develop the plant's capability for JIT delivery.

Much of the subsequent work focused on shop-floor improvements. In the existing plant layout, machines were arranged by function, with one hundred assembly workstations placed in rows around an inspection room at the centre of the factory floor. It was clear that cost savings and JIT delivery could not be achieved with this layout. The simplifications being planned for various production processes would require that benches, machine tools, quality control workstations and areas for storage and staging all be rearranged. Eventually, the plant was converted to operate as an FMC with the original inspection room being replaced by a central area for planning and control that included equipment for tooling and calibration. Aside from speeding the movement of WIP, the new arrangement allowed for an improved means of visible control.

Training, process simplification and improvement in the plant layout were only some of the adjustments that were necessary. The rigours of JIT manufacturing meant that shipping arrangements, methods of inventory replenishment, production schedules and manufacturing lead times all had to be coordinated between this plant and its customers and suppliers. The firm set out to accomplish this task by specifying a series of specific targets or milestones:

- **Determine customers' requirements and improve service**. The firm's overall plan for improvement had to be successfully implemented. At the same time, teams of operating managers received special training to meet the needs of the customer.

- **Acquire first orders**. Customers had to be convinced that the firm clearly understood their requirements and could satisfy them.

- **Start prototype manufacture**. The customer's engineers and buyers had to be included in the plant's improvement teams. With their help, manufacturing processes and production schedules could be fine-tuned to meet the customer's requirements.

- **Produce the first article**. With the new manufacturing processes in place, the firm had to demonstrate that the customer's standards for quality could be met.

- **Start pre-production manufacturing**. At this stage the customer's acceptance of the new methods for production, reporting and statistical process control was needed. The customer must also be convinced of the plant's ability to produce the required quality and volume of product. Finally, binding commitments from Elamex's own suppliers had to be obtained.

- **Deliver the first production lot**. Ensure that delivery meets the JIT specifications of the customer.

- **Reconfirm production routines**. Determine that there is complete compliance with routines and commitments governing quantity, production schedules and quality.

- **Begin full production**. JIT production becomes a reality and the plant is prepared to win new contracts in a more demanding environment.

This detailed sequence of steps followed by Elamex underlines the importance of commitment, planning and persistence.  Though it was easy to recognize the need for change and to set ambitious goals, managers' true challenge is to coordinate all this work and guide the firm through the endless detail that is a necessary part of the improvement process.  The involvement of customers and suppliers complicated the task in the early stages, but in the longer run their presence makes the transition easier and the probability of success higher.  After much work and many improvements, this particular plant became a certified supplier to several of the world's largest electronics manufacturers.

In conclusion, the principles described here are rigorously followed in plants producing a wide variety of products for dissimilar customers.  An intimate knowledge of customers and a constant dedication to improvement is essential in all cases.  Once managers understand their customers' requirements and are serious about applying continuous improvement, teams should be formed to accomplish certain broad tasks.  First, they must analyse and understand each manufacturing process and then come up with an overall plan for improvement.  Second, they must bring the manufacturing processes under control with tools such as SPC.  Wherever possible, this will be accomplished by simplifying these processes.  Third, they must always strive to reduce throughput time in order to cut costs, improve quality and speed delivery.  Finally, teams do not consider technological enhancements (such as computer control systems or automated equipment) until the process is understood and brought under control.  Cost-effective improvements through process simplification are always the first alternative.

## CONCLUSIONS AND IMPRESSIONS

The case studies presented here provide the basis for some generalizations which support views expressed in previous chapters.  First, some observers have argued that methods of continuous improvement are uniquely suited to certain cultures, particularly those of Japan and some other Asian countries.  They go on to assume that the same procedures may be less appropriate for use in other parts of the world.  That interpretation is refuted by the experiences summarized here and by a much larger body of evidence compiled by other investigators.  Many of the techniques are so simple and basic as to be nearly universal in their application.  Furthermore, the fact that successful CIFs emphasize cooperation and a collective approach to change fits well with many local cultures.

Second, the case studies reconfirm the results of more wide-ranging research which points to the crucial role of management in promoting continuous improvement. Managers' contribution to these programmes could be particularly important in developing countries where levels of experience and education of production-line workers are often low. Employee involvement is also essential, but without the commitment of managers, any programme of continuous improvement will flounder.

Third, our research shows that improvements in production systems can yield very substantial savings. The same point has been argued by Juran and others who emphasize that the greatest potential for gains in efficiency and quality can be achieved by focusing attention on the production system. This possibility is especially relevant for manufacturers in developing countries where capital shortages and foreign exchange constraints make other forms of improvement and modernization difficult. Continuous improvement is not a proprietary form of technology like most types of advanced equipment. The cost of acquisition is low and the great emphasis it places on workers and workers' skills is compatible with the economic and social goals of most developing countries.

Fourth, industry's record in developing countries is marred by repeated instances where firms operate as 'enclaves' or industrial outposts with no links or benefits for the local community. CIFs, with their emphasis on JIT, customers' requirements and workers' skills, can not afford to be isolated from the local economy. Part of these firms' philosophy is to create a community of employee 'stakeholders' who are committed to the company, the customer and continuous improvement. The vitality of the local economy is essential since this is where the CIF trades and recruits the employees which are so crucial to its prosperity.

Finally, a firm's ability to master continuous improvement does not require a minimum size or scale of operations. Both small and large manufacturers are capable of using these techniques. In fact, small firms may even have some advantages over their larger counterparts. In small firms the management is much closer to production. Teamwork, information sharing, and other hallmarks of continuous improvement are easier to implement in firms with fewer employees and managers on the shop floor. Additional layers of management in larger enterprises will extend the time required to shift to continuous improvement production.

In another sense, small firms may be at a disadvantage. They will not always be able to create the intensive programmes for internal training we have described here. It will be important that they join forces with policy makers and local training institutions. Higher-level training, whether for small or large enterprises, can benefit from subregional cooperation. Chambers of Commerce and similar organizations can play a catalytic and coordinating role in this particular field. So, too, can major foreign investors. Concerns such as these fall into the realm of policy and are discussed in the following chapter.

# NOTES

1.  This case study relies heavily on Walker (1988) and other materials supplied by Packard Electric International. Additional information was obtained by UNIDO staff through interviews and plant tours of Packard's Mexican operations. Several individuals generously offered their advice and opinions. Mark D. Sabau, Manager of Mexican Operations was especially helpful in providing important data and allowing UNIDO staff access to all of his facilities. He and his staff provided much insight into the process of continuous improvement in developing countries. Special thanks also go to John Wyko, Robert Saviers, Rafael Marroquin, Jesús Ceniceros, Miguel Cázares, Hector Martinez, Rafael López, Reynaldo Cervantes, Jim Faflick, Jesús Medina Concha, Salvador Flores, Thomas Goodman, and many others at Packard International-Mexican Operations.
2.  Packard Electric International is affiliated with General Motors. Its Mexican operations serve many multinationals, most of them with multiple plants in Europe and North America. These include: BMW, Freightliner Truck, Mercedes Benz, Siemens, Sumitomo, Suzuki, GM-Toyota, and Saturn-GM. Packard Mexico's JIT deliveries are to the NUMMI plant (GM-Toyota) in Fremont, California, the Saturn (GM) plant in Spring Hill, Tennessee and the Suzuki plant in Ingersoll, Ontario.
3.  These stress marks resulted from use of a small rosebud clip during the assembly process. Packard's engineers thought the marks were innocuous since they had no effect on performance. However, they were the reason for an extended confrontation between the two firms. Toyota engineers insisted that the marks were not specified in the NUMMI blueprints and the frustrated team of Packard engineers eventually agreed. The following day, Toyota's team returned with a blueprint for a design which prevented stress marks (Walker, 1988, p. 3).
4.  Another of Packard's visual controls is a card which holds wiring clips used in the assembly of harnesses. The clips are mounted on cards with each row corresponding to the exact number required per harness. By glancing at the card, operators can quickly see if a clip is missing from a harness and what type it is. This simple device is more effective than expensive electronic checking systems. Another visual aid is used on the cabinets where dies are stored. A magnet identifies the die size and position in the cabinet. When the dies are in the compartment, blue magnets are put on the door. A green magnet signifies that the die is in use on a press, while a red magnet means the die is being serviced or replacement parts are on order.
5.  For instance, on the same day that a General Motors official praised the orderliness of the Packard plant, one of the engineers from Sumitomo presented a list of 38 items which were considered serious housekeeping deficiencies.
6.  Operators are provided with the training and procedures necessary to make such decisions. This is an excellent example of an instance where the removal of a buffer or other non-value-adding cushion reveals substantial variation in the manufacturing process.
7.  In one instance, an improvement team achieved impressive results in a particular manufacturing process by moving two sets of machines to adjacent positions and rearranging the sub assembly tables. Their objective was to enable multiskilled operators to move more material with the same effort. These alterations were quickly carried out and the results were measured and posted. Once the changes were introduced, 7 operators were able to perform the same tasks previously done by 12. Walking distances were slashed by 96 per cent, the lead time for materials used in this particular process was reduced from 7.5 days to 1 hour, and inventory was cut from 13 days to one shift. In another example, a simple rearrangement of machinery reduced both the rate of defectives and the

amount of necessary floor space by 50 per cent, cut lead times by 46 per cent and slashed inventory by 33 per cent.

8.  Two minor operations — placing rubber gaskets on the valve seats and inserting nuts on the control bolts — were not included in the analysis of this process since they can be done at other times and are used to balance the workload during later steps in the assembly process.

9.  One of these recommendations was partial mechanization of several operations. Another was to double the number of workstations used in the assembly line. Both required significant additional investments and were not considered. A third proposal called for additional equipment to accelerate the inspection procedures at workstation 5. Team members noted that the time required for inspection was mainly a function of the operating time of the machinery used. The existing apparatus for testing was outmoded and managers agreed to include the purchase of new equipment in their investment plan.

10.  This case study is based on a more extensive analysis of companies in the United Republic of Tanzania carried out by Paul Hesp and Masayoshi Matsushita, Regional and Country Studies Branch, UNIDO.

11.  Expatriates are the Managing Director who doubles as Director of Finance and Administration, a Director of Marketing and a Director of Planning and Production who also serves as Director of Battery Production and the Manager of Radio Production.

12.  The company's minimum wage is slightly above the average for all manufacturers, though less than offered by most parastatals. One of the firm's advantages is that wages are paid regularly (which is not always the case in other companies). Another is the generous range of services it offers, including free lunches, transport and health care.

13.  New equipment (again from Japan) is to be installed during 1993–94, possibly with some Japanese government support. However, the main source of finance for the expansion is the subsidiary's own foreign exchange earnings.

14.  This case study was prepared by Nicolas Phillips, Director of Engineering and Technology for Elamex, S.A. Dr. Phillips is in charge of Elamex's programmes in Industrial and Manufacturing Systems Engineering, Environmental Management and Quality Management.

15.  The firm recently received an advanced quality certification from the British Standards Institute.

16.  Start-up operations may obviously find it cheaper to create a series of FMCs than firms or plants that are already in operation. Firms that design their new plants to operate in this manner are often able to undercut competitors working in older factories. Elamex's managers experienced such a case when they were asked to bid on a contract to assemble wiring harnesses. They knew that the customer's own manufacturing process required 300 direct labour operators. After redesigning the operation, Elamex determined that it could reduce the number of workers by a third and based its bid on this workforce. Elamex lost the contract to a new plant of another company which was able to do the same job with only 49 operators. There were no significant differences between the two firms' technologies. The outcome was mainly determined by the fact that Elamex's rival had a new plant which was originally designed to work according to FMC and to make use of an advanced system of visible controls.

17.  Production-line balance is largely determined by the speed of the conveyor and the number of steps performed by each operator. It must be continuously monitored to ensure that work is evenly distributed between each workstation. Operator fatigue, differences in efficiency and the ability to meet quality requirements must also be taken into account.

# 7. Problems and Prospects

Firms that successfully implement programmes of continuous improvement can look forward to substantial gains in productivity and efficiency. Given the potential benefits, we might expect to find some of these techniques in almost any manufacturing plant, whether it is located in an industrialized or a developing country. Yet that is clearly not the case. One disturbing feature is that few companies in developing countries have embraced this option. Manufacturers in industrialized countries are proving to be willing experimenters — perhaps because they are more exposed to the pressures of international competition — but their counterparts in developing countries have been slow to adopt the same techniques. Ironically, it is the latter firms that probably stand to gain the most from continuous improvement. Another concern is that the success rate for all new practitioners appears to be modest. The evidence on this point is anecdotal, although a substantial number of firms that have turned to continuous improvement have been disappointed by the results.[1]

Some of these obstacles are unique to the developing countries while others are common to firms in any part of the world. The more important barriers which exist within the firm are described in the following section. Other hindrances and options for promoting continuous improvement that are discussed in this chapter include: the interrelationship between culture and managerial styles, the role of public policy, priorities for education and vocational training and actions which individual firms can take to promote continuous improvement.

## BARRIERS TO IMPLEMENTATION WITHIN THE FIRM

Entrenched resistance and managerial indifference are two of the most common obstacles. The main source of opposition may be managers, workers or both but the most formidable barriers to improvement originate in the top echelons of management (Mogab and Bós, 1992). Many senior executives are extremely impatient, defining success purely in terms of its impact on short-term financial indicators.[2] Their predilection for near-instant results suggests they do not fully understand or accept the principles of continuous improvement. Such a simplistic view can quickly breed more confusion as managers are likely to assume that specific tools — for example, quality control circles or statistical process control — are synonymous with the overall process of continuous improvement (Yoshida, 1989). But when particular tools are used in isolation from other components, the outcome is likely to be negative and discredit the entire programme.

A managerial attitude of indifference can be just as damaging. When senior executives choose to delegate the responsibility for improvement activities to subordinates, these programmes become another specialized function rather than the overarching concern for the entire firm. In effect, managers are signalling that they have more important things to do, or that they do not understand improvement activities. A general waning of interest and a lack of support for the improvement programmes soon follows — particularly if these activities are not immediately translated into higher profits.

Continuous improvement necessarily requires that the role of almost every member of the firm be altered. The heavy reliance on informal information and shop-floor innovations are some of the major reasons for this change. If improvement programmes are to succeed, production-line workers must be given greater responsibility. It follows that other members of the firm will lose some measure of responsibility and authority. Middle managers and supervisors are typically the losers and may vigorously oppose the use of CITs.

More broadly-based resistance emerges when managers use improvement programmes as a means of shedding workers and eliminating layers of management. This tactic is a common one in industrialized countries, although it runs counter to the principles on which continuous improvement is based.[3] Suspicious employees are disinclined to share production information and may actively oppose any attempts to introduce improvements on the shop floor. In fact, all forms of innovation and planning become more difficult when individuals fear that their best efforts could cost their jobs.

How can aspiring CIFs deal with these internal obstacles? Without the unequivocal support of top managers, any of these programmes will flounder. But a strong commitment by managers is not enough. They must also know how to improve flexibility, productivity and quality. To deal with workers' concern about security, managers must make it abundantly clear that improvement efforts will not result in job losses. It is inevitable that firms must sometimes reduce their workforce. If possible, this phase should be completed before embarking on such a programme. Workers with a measure of security and job certainty will not only be more open to continuous improvement but are more likely to acquire valuable firm-specific knowledge.

# THE MANAGEMENT GAP

The fact that some managers do not provide the support and leadership which improvement programmes demand may reflect a widespread shortage of people with the requisite supervisory experience and skills. This scarcity of managerial talent is a general barrier to continuous improvement and discourages the inflow of direct foreign investment which can transmit these skills. Much of the managerial experience that exists in developing countries is gained in public enterprises, multinational corporations or family-run firms, and each of these organizational forms is discussed here.

Governments in many developing countries have begun to reduce their ownership of and control over manufacturing enterprises. Yet the size of the public sector remains large and its legacy for modern-day managers is great (Perkins, 1991). Publicly-owned companies typically draw from a small pool of potential managers. This group may be highly educated, but many are political appointees with little management experience. Nor are they likely to gain managerial experience in a state-run enterprise. Such firms are slow to change and possess no system which allows managers to learn from their mistakes. Major decisions are often taken by government officials and the firm's senior manager then administers them in a 'top-down' fashion.

The possibility that some of the techniques described in this book would be considered for use in such companies is remote. Publicly-owned firms in developing countries rarely have any means to determine whether their outputs are actually meeting the intended results (Seckler and Nobe, 1983). Meanwhile, their managers tend to identify with the government agency or political group that is mainly responsible for their appointment. Neither of these characteristics will be conducive to the development of improvement programmes.

Another potential source of managerial expertise is the multinational corporation. These firms' preference for local sourcing, coupled with their ample experience in continuous improvement and the large number of subsidiaries which exist in developing countries, make them a useful channel for the international transfer of improvement skills. That option has certain limitations, however. One is that much of the multinationals' investment is concentrated in a small number of developing countries and in specific fields of manufacturing. Another is that multinationals pay more generous salaries than most local firms and it is difficult to lure these managers away. Finally, some of the world's leading CIFs are reluctant to use many local personnel in managerial positions. The opportunities for domestic employees to master elements of continuous improvement and other modern management techniques may be constrained by limits placed on their upward mobility (see Box 7.1).

Many manufacturing firms in developing countries are family-run. These companies are usually small and their managers are not far removed from the production line. Such conditions should offer numerous opportunities to rely on shop-floor improvements, though most evidence suggests that family firms are inclined toward management practices that are inimical to continuous improvement. Research in Brazil (where 95 per cent of registered firms are family-run) indicates that a majority of owner-managers operate in a paternalistic manner. They are surrounded by an inner circle of relatives and friends which has nothing to do with abilities or professional competence. Most members of the group remain with the firm for a long time, although the turnover of line staff and workers is high. Not surprisingly, family firms that operate in highly protected markets have a long life expectancy and show little inclination to alter their existing managerial style (Bós, 1993). When exposed to fast-changing markets, many of these will be among the first to disappear. Whatever their fate, it is clear that such conditions are not likely to produce a cadre of managers who are open to methods of continuous improvement.

In summary, manufacturers in developing countries may have great difficulty finding managers and supervisors with any training or experience which is relevant for improvement programmes. None of these firms — state-owned, family-run or even multinationals — serve as a good breeding ground for the necessary management skills. Firms in developing countries will often be forced to consider other options in order to assemble the necessary skills to implement continuous improvement.

---

**Box 7.1   Local managers as a conduit for continuous improvement**

Multinationals that rely on continuous improvement in their country of origin are sometimes reluctant to employ many local people as managers in their overseas subsidiaries. When such a hiring practice is widely followed, it raises questions about the multinational's ability to sustain programmes for continuous improvement in its foreign subsidiaries. Managers of some multinationals' plants in developing countries report that they have had to discontinue many of the improvement practices that established their firms as world leaders. In Mexico, there is evidence that foreign multinationals have actually reverted to more traditional methods, such as heavy reliance on inspection procedures, to ensure that quality levels are maintained.

It is possible that locally recruited workers, when they realize that their chances for promotion are limited, will not be motivated to expend the extra effort required for continuous improvement. For further discussion, see Wilson, 1992; Shaiken and Browne, 1991; Bós, 1991; and Fucini and Fucini, 1990.

# THE IMPACT OF CULTURE ON MANAGEMENT[4]

The question of whether continuous improvement is suitable in some cultures but not others has been briefly noted in earlier chapters. Our own view is that the performance of employees is mainly determined not by cultural traits but by the organization in which they work. With access to the same set of tools and knowledge, people from different cultures tend to perform similarly in similar organizations — and people from similar cultures will perform differently in different types of organizations (Seckler and Nobe, 1983). Furthermore, the objectives of continuous improvement are universal. Measurable and ongoing improvements in manufacturing process and products are not culturally relative.

Culture does enter into the discussion in a narrower sense, however. Managerial style is a product of the individual's culture (Trompenaars, 1993). There are probably several different management styles that are compatible with the principles of continuous improvement, though the most effective style will depend on the culture of the firm's workforce. An achievement-oriented managerial style has been assumed throughout this book, but two other versions — the ascriptive and the paternalistic manager — are also common and are briefly discussed here.

Ascriptive cultures assign a high value to social prestige. Individuals are rewarded on the basis of kinship, family position, gender or age, personal contacts, educational level and similar criteria. This approach can lead to quite different results from an achievement-oriented system where individuals receive recognition according to an objective record of their performance. For example, an individual in an achievement-oriented culture is likely to be asked what he studied, whereas in an ascriptive culture the same person would be asked where he studied (Trompenaars, 1993, p. 10).

The ascriptive manager spends a great deal of time and energy building networks of allies and supporters. Members of the firm who share the manager's attributes are the ones receiving promotions and other organizational awards. Such a style does not preclude the option of continuous improvement but when senior managers base their decisions predominantly on ascriptive criteria, there is little possibility that these programmes can succeed. Ascriptive-oriented management is common among firms in both the public and private sector in many developing countries.

Paternalism is one of the oldest forms of human organization and often goes hand in hand with an ascriptive style of management. It refers to the behaviour of a superior towards a subordinate — in much the same way that a father relates to his child. Such relationships assume many forms but the tacit assumption underlying paternalism is that the subordinate lacks power and knowledge and therefore needs the help and protection of the more experienced and competent superior. Aid and security are provided by the paternalistic manager in return for unquestioning loyalty, respect, and cooperation of the subordinate. Such a managerial style is found in family firms, in many small and medium-sized firms and in a number of public enterprises and bureaucracies.

Paternalistic managers are resistant to change and tend to be intolerant or sceptical of new methods and procedures. Their firms are very tightly run, with rigid administration from above and rules to govern every type of procedure. If certain actions are not explicitly permitted, members of the firm will generally assume that they are prohibited. Criticism and information flows from top management downward and any questioning of authority is defined as insubordination.

Such an environment influences the behaviour of the entire workforce. Middle managers, production-line supervisors and shop-floor workers tend to be 'risk averse', meaning that they are reluctant to take any actions which have an uncertain outcome. Virtually all members of the firm refrain from making suggestions about ways to improve production processes. Instead, their attention is focused on matters relating to production inputs and a premium is placed on the adherence to carefully designed production plans. Change becomes very difficult in such paternalistic enterprises and any external shock (for example, an important technological innovation) can trigger endless power struggles. Unfortunately, these struggles usually pit one paternalistic manager against another. Such disputes lead to the active suppression and control of information which is seen as a possible weapon against perceived enemies. The main concern of the protagonists is with power rather than organizational performance (Seckler and Nobe, 1983, pp. 288–91).

Neither ascriptive nor paternalistic enterprises would seem to provide a healthy setting for continuous improvement. Upward mobility is constrained, middle management and production-line workers have little decision-making responsibility and information flows mainly from top to bottom. Yet many of the undesirable characteristics exhibited by these types of firms are shared with mass production manufacturers. And it is the mass production firms which account for the largest number of new recruits to continuous improvement. The most important characteristic determining the success of an improvement programme is that the senior executives — regardless of cultural influences — are committed to a system that provides incentives for sustained improvement. Once committed, all managers will be confronted by new roles and challenges that will change the way a firm operates.

Supporting evidence for this view comes from Japan, where both ascriptive and paternalistic management styles were commonplace in the period when continuous improvement first took hold. That heritage is readily apparent today in the way many of these firms are organized and operate. Job security, consensual decision-making, systems for promotion and reward are based on characteristics other than performance. Links between suppliers and their customers are only some of the Japanese characteristics that fit into the ascriptive or paternalistic mould. Other examples are the senior managers' insistence on the notion of a 'company family' and the fact that subordinates participate in both the duties and privileges of family members. All major plans and policies emanate from the highest levels of the organization, being interpreted and translated into concrete action plans at each level of seniority.

While similarities between management styles in the developing countries and Japan should not be overlooked, important differences remain. Decisions in Japanese companies are sometimes biased in favour of ascriptive or paternalistic criteria but the consequences tend to be specified and are increasingly contractual. The loyalty and commitment of workers is invested in the organization rather than in a paternal leader who dispenses favours. Most important, top management assumes responsibility for creating and maintaining a system that encourages ongoing improvements.

In conclusion, culture does influence managers, though it need not stifle the improvement process. Nor does there appear to be any single best cultural predisposition for managers who wish to implement such programmes.[5] Improvement efforts flourish in an environment of cooperation — which may fit well with many cultures in the developing world that display a strong collectivist orientation. It is also possible that continuous improvement methods are more appropriate to such cultures than mass production methods such as performance appraisals and management by objectives (UNIDO, 1991, p. 9).

## THE ROLE OF GOVERNMENT AND PUBLIC POLICY

Productivity gains are an essential part of any country's long-term efforts to raise standards of living. Firms must constantly search for ways to increase productivity through every means possible. At the same time, they need to develop the capability to move into new and more sophisticated fields where levels of productivity are generally higher (Porter, 1990, Chapter 1).

The policy environment in developing countries is not always conducive to these sorts of developments. Many public officials ascribe to a view of economic growth which holds that productivity gains depend largely on rates of capital accumulation. The consequences of this view are readily apparent in the policy mix of a typical developing country (see Chapter 2). The availability of capital is clearly a critical growth stimulant, but there is abundant evidence which indicates that rates of capital accumulation do not explain satisfactorily why some countries enjoy faster rates of economic growth than others. Instead, it is the different ways that a country's economic agents use all their productive inputs which determines international differences in economic performance. Examples include a broad range of improvements in the capabilities of managers and workers and more effective ways to use existing plants, equipment and other resources (see Perkins, 1991, pp.11–54). Options such as these will have a greater impact on the overall pattern of productivity growth than the indiscriminate accumulation of capital.

A policy maker's neglect of microeconomic matters can also hinder the development of improvement programmes. Governments in every country can point to a variety of policies they have adopted to encourage economic growth. Prominent examples are measures to encourage privatization, exchange rate policies to alter the prices of imports and exports (for example, devaluation), high tariff walls and non-tariff barriers to shut out imports, tax reforms, methods of dispersing credit and foreign exchange allocation to favoured industries and programmes to encourage exports. A primary objective of these policies is to attain some competitive advantage by exploiting the availability of natural resources or cheap labour, by altering prices through policy means, or by shutting out foreign competition.

However, productivity growth and higher living standards are unlikely to be attained through measures that do not encourage firms to take initiatives on their own. One drawback is the implicit assumption that managers will always choose the most appropriate combination of technologies and inputs from among all those available. Such foresight would be rare even in the most sophisticated economies. Another danger is that any competitive advantage created by such policies tends to be transient or inherently unstable. The same tactics can be easily imitated by other countries and any competitive advantage is quickly eroded.

The sorts of policies and initiatives that are meant to encourage microeconomic advances may take longer to bring results, but the benefits they yield are lasting ones. First, they will be cost-effective since they allow firms to develop a wide range of competitive capabilities without the need for massive government support. Second, productivity gains and similar forms of progress will not be undermined by inflation or erratic shifts in exchange rates. Finally, this 'internal' impetus for productivity growth and development of competitive prowess provides the strong base for new business formation that can be translated into a healthy and growing industrial base. Such a policy orientation is especially important in developing countries that have yet to develop a wide range of manufacturing capabilities and where government ownership or control has overshadowed the influence of the private sector.

Policy, however, is no substitute for the dedication of managers and firms. Programmes of continuous improvement can only succeed through the efforts of the firms themselves. Governments — even those staffed by highly qualified and dedicated civil servants — have been notoriously unsuccessful in managing firms and in responding to rapid changes in market conditions. Public officials are rarely in tune with market forces and are influenced by many political considerations that bear little relevance for objective improvement.

Policy makers in developing countries can encourage the implementation of continuous improvement by offering greater support to the development of management and technical resources and by upgrading labour skills. Such a shift will necessarily mean that less resources are spent to defray the costs of capital and encourage capital accumulation. However, the implicit assumption that managers will naturally adopt the most efficient methods of production and organizational forms if only they are provided with the proper equipment and facilities does not hold up to scrutiny in most cases.

## EDUCATION AND TRAINING

In order to promote continuous improvement, government officials must make adjustments in educational programmes at the primary, secondary, vocational and university levels. These moves are essential since the cost of training and education can not be borne by a majority of enterprises in developing countries. Special efforts may be required at the university level. Public funding for education in many developing countries tends to be overwhelmingly biased in favour of upper-income groups and offers limited support for science, mathematics, engineering, statistics and related fields which are so important for continuous improvement (see Box 7.2).

Technical universities and vocational schools are an especially critical part of any nation-wide programme of continuous improvement. These institutions stress practical applications and their faculties are knowledgeable about the industrial environment. They can be a prime vehicle to promote statistical quality control, total productive maintenance, quality design and other improvements in products and production processes. Government officials can assist by encouraging technical and vocational schools to cooperate closely with industry and to maintain continuous contacts with companies. Policy makers can intervene directly by encouraging a variety of cooperative arrangements between universities, vocational and technical institutions, businesses and research bodies. Among the options available, the following are some of the most promising:

---

**Box 7.2   The need to redirect public spending priorities for education**

Public expenditures per student are naturally higher for university students than for those at the primary and secondary levels. But in many developing countries the imbalance in spending patterns is extreme. For example, figures gathered by the United Nations and the World Bank indicate that in some developing countries the typical university student receives up to 90 times as much in public money as each primary and secondary student. This bias reflects the fact that almost all university graduates come from upper-income groups which wield considerable political influence. The result is that a vast majority of the country's workforce gets little public support for their basic education. Later, these students go on to become factory workers and may be ill-prepared in programmes for improvement and total quality control.

University professors in developing countries also have a predilection for theory over practice and prefer to remain aloof from the real-world problems occurring on the factory floor. Their training and capabilities are seldom brought to bear in fields such as continuous improvement. These attitudes are reflected in the material covered in many courses. Deming, for example, notes that university-level statistics courses rarely provide any training in statistical quality control — despite its widespread use and importance. Instead, students are expected to master material which is important in the formal study of statistics. Such an approach provides neither a basis for action, nor the ability to predict results of the next experiment. Yet both these attributes are critical for process and product improvement (Deming, 1982, pp. 67–8).

---

- A range of apprenticeships, internships, and schemes for on-the-job training which provide experience in the practical application of CITs.

- The use of visiting instructors from industry, including consultants and employees of local subsidiaries and affiliates of multinationals, to teach methods and techniques of continuous improvement.

- Strong links between research groups in universities and private companies which stress applied research on new methods of continuous improvement.

- Collaboration between universities and industrial and trade associations on strategies relating to continuous improvement.

- Creation of permanent training centres based in universities.

Apprenticeships and internships provide students with the opportunity to combine formal instruction in methods of continuous improvement with on-the-job training.[6] The host firms can evaluate prospective employees and get cost-effective suggestions on ways to improve shop-floor procedures. Meanwhile, the institutions strengthen their links with individual companies and stay abreast of new developments in industry. Government support — for example, various types of subsidies or tax breaks to employers or schools — may be necessary in most developing countries when programmes for apprenticeships or internships are first launched. Over time, employers should recognize the value of these programmes and support can be withdrawn.

The effectiveness of training can be greatly enhanced by bringing experts and practitioners from private industry into the classroom. In many developing countries this resource is overlooked by educational institutions.[7] Yet, local firms and multinational corporations may possess a rich reservoir of talent and experience in the field of continuous improvement and quality control. The visitors can conduct workshops and seminars on specific topics and applied problems, as well as serving as guest speakers to augment formal classes. Such expertise is based on practical experience rather than academic credentials and helps students to identify the most effective techniques from a wider range of theoretical alternatives. Because most CITs are developed by industrial specialists rather than academics, practitioners tend to be more up to date in the use of the latest techniques.

Governments in developing countries may have to initiate these interchanges. State-funded educational institutions should be nudged in the direction of more interchange with the private sector.[8] Local industries must be encouraged to offer their employees classroom training (possibly with subsidies or tax breaks). If the government makes its support for the national diffusion of continuous improvement evident — perhaps by establishing national awards akin to the Deming Prize in Japan or the Baldridge Award in the United States — firms will be more willing to voluntarily support local educational institutions. Such support can also be a condition for investment by foreign multinationals.

Leading industries in many developing countries are often associated with specialized research institutes or specific academic departments in universities. Government support for those centres dedicated to applied methods of continuous improvement can have significant pay-offs. Funds may be reallocated away from government laboratories which have a poor record of success in order to support commercial applications. Public officials can also encourage research with commercial implications by providing matching funds or underwriting the costs of contracts between industry and university research institutes.

An even more effective approach is to establish permanent university-based centres dedicated to training managers, technicians and workers in the application of CITs.[9] UNIDO is currently assisting in the creation of such centres in Brazil and Hungary. They can be staffed by full- or part-time faculty with plant-level experience in applied methods of quality control and continuous improvement. Training sessions and seminars should also include quality and improvement professionals from multinational firms as well as their national counterparts. Government support is required in the start-up phase. However, these centres are ultimately expected to be self-financing (usually within three years) through funds obtained from trade and industry associations and chambers of commerce, as well as fees paid by individual firms.

Creation of a permanent centre can be an invaluable step in promoting and disseminating methods of continuous improvement in a developing country. A major advantage is that customized courses can be developed for specific industries and firms. A more effective balance between classroom training and on-site assistance also becomes possible. Staff are expected to visit clients' plants and assist in the implementation and monitoring of techniques. Finally, a permanent centre will be able to address the strategic aspects of continuous improvement which firms or short-term experts can not.

Aside from these advantages, a permanent institution avoids some of the pitfalls commonly encountered with other methods for training and application. First, they will generally be cheaper than consultants and their training more appropriate than that offered by universities. Second, consulting firms tend to specialize in a limited range of CITs which may not be appropriate for the changing needs of the firms. A permanent centre is better able to meet these varied and changing needs. Third, assistance from consultants is almost always limited in duration, although the transition from a beginning practitioner to a CIF takes many years. Fourth, a permanent centre is better prepared to advise on many of the strategic issues of continuous improvement which are of a long-term character and link suppliers with their customers (see Box 7.3). Finally, these centres can afford to take a very practical approach to improvement problems while universities (and sometimes consultants) emphasize theoretical aspects rather than applications.

## PROMOTING CONTINUOUS IMPROVEMENT IN THE FIRM

Firms, rather than countries or governments, are on the front lines of the competitive struggle and will need to do everything possible to ensure that their improvement programmes succeed. There are several steps manufacturers in developing countries can take to improve their chances of success. Costs are associated with each step but should be regarded as a necessary investment in the productive capabilities of the firm.

**Box 7.3 Strategic and long-term issues for promotion of continuous improvement**

A permanent centre dedicated to training and dissemination of the techniques of continuous improvement is the only institutional option which can handle certain aspects of a widely-based programme. Because each centre is expected to be self-financing, it must have close contacts with trade and industry associations as well as the larger firms in the developing country. This network is a great advantage when dealing with certain issues.

For example, there may be widespread agreement that JIT manufacturing represents a desirable step for most members of a particular industry. However, the move requires the active participation of suppliers; they must be able to produce relatively defect-free lots of materials in specified amounts and make them available at agreed times. Without this capability, the best efforts of the downstream manufacturers will not succeed. A permanent centre can work with chambers of commerce and trade and industry associations to gain support for the widespread adoption of JIT. Later, it can provide the specific types of training and long-term support that such a programme would require.

Top executives and their staffs must be familiar with the techniques of continuous improvement and be personally involved. Senior managers need to be trained before the firm can embark on a programme of this sort. This group is often so immersed in the day-to-day routine of business that the connection between production processes and the end goal of customer satisfaction is lost. Improvement-based strategies for long-term growth must be based on a clear sense of how the firm intends to serve the customer. Managers will have to develop an entirely new set of priorities. These are taken very seriously and are discussed thoroughly at an early stage during executive training.

Managers must also understand the role of statistical variation and how the basic statistical methods (control charts, graphs and other tools of continuous improvement) are used. They need to be familiar with the experiences of other firms and able to adapt these experiences to their own situation. Middle managers will ultimately have to function as trainers or group leaders and will be expected to train subordinates in the use of CITs. These tasks are more difficult than issuing direct orders: all middle managers will need training to prepare them for their new responsibilities.

Training should begin with a one to two week course of full-time study for senior and middle managers outside the plant. Ideally, these courses would take place in an institute which specializes in continuous improvement and related disciplines. If a permanent institute does not exist nearby, or if managers can not leave the plant, outside consultants and trainers may have to be brought in.

This option can be expensive and the range of instruction may be limited. Alternatively, there are many useful books (often widely translated) and videos which can be used in-house. While motivated managers can learn much through self-study (see, for example, the suggested readings at the end of this chapter) certain topics like statistical process control are better mastered when taught by qualified instructors. All managers should consider themselves students of continuous improvement and participate in self-study and in-house training on a continuous basis.[10]

Supervisors, foremen, technicians and engineers must thoroughly master the tools of continuous improvement. Training for this group will focus less on strategy and more on shop-level techniques such as reductions in set-up time, TPM and the design and operation of cellular processes. Engineers should receive training in SPC and more advanced techniques.[11] Supervisors and foremen require guidance in group dynamics, communications skills, team work and training skills as they will participate in self-managed and semi-autonomous work teams such as quality control circles.

While group and team work is well suited to capture important information and ideas direct from workers, these activities will alter the traditional roles of middle managers, supervisors and foremen. Supervisors working in developing countries do not normally seek consultation or suggestions from subordinates. Once improvement activities begin in earnest, supervisory personnel have a crucial role to play within the improvement groups. They must foster worker creativity and train their workers to use the tools of continuous improvement. These new duties will prove difficult and need to be supported by long-term training.

Workers on the production line will also have difficult adjustments to make as programmes of continuous improvement enter the factory. Rather than specializing in a narrow set of routines, they will have to function as generalists performing a variety of tasks. The statistical and analytical tools they use will be unfamiliar at first but are an integral part of the overall programme. At the same time, attitudes and relations on the shop floor will also have to change; collaboration will be a prominent part of the new environment. All these adjustments will be difficult, but the workers that successfully make the transition will be more productive and more satisfied with their jobs.

One of the first goals of training programmes for production-line workers is to overcome the resistance to change on the shop floor. Workers who have been accustomed to following orders will be confused and uneasy when confronted with new roles and expectations. Some will feel threatened by their new jobs and reluctant to cooperate with others. These fears should be allayed at an early stage. Workers should also be reassured that continuous improvement will not lead to job losses.

The subject matter covered during the initial training of production-line workers includes the basic analytical tools, the role of external and internal customers, the importance of statistical variation and the use of data in decision-making. Later, more complicated subjects such as data collection and the use of control charts and graphs can be introduced through formal courses and on-the-job training. Courses should be constantly improved and adapted to meet the specific needs of workers, with the more experienced employees conducting in-house courses for newcomers. Much thought needs to be given to the content of these courses, methods of presentation, the sequence of material to be presented and the timing (see Box 7.4).

The scope of training in developing countries may have to go beyond matters of continuous improvement. Many entry-level workers possess low levels of literacy and numeracy and have no previous experience in manufacturing. These shortcomings are an obstacle but need not impede shop-floor improvements. With in-house training, such workers have repeatedly proven themselves competent in carrying out all the basic elements of SPC and data analysis.

---

**Box 7.4   Principles and techniques for in-plant training**

One of the first steps in an in-plant training programme is for managers to set up some procedures to 'train trainers'. One advantage is that personnel who study to become trainers learn much more than passive students. Such an approach also provides an early indicator of key individuals' aptitudes and abilities to use CITs and helps to generate new ideas for improvement.

Other important considerations concern the size of classes and the length of time they run. Providing training to large groups of workers over long periods of time is not efficient. The most effective courses will be offered 'just-in-time', or just prior to their actual application (Muther and Lytle, 1992, pp. 103–13). For example, rather than exposing inexperienced line workers to several hours of instruction, a short session might stress a single tool or application. Immediately following the session, the worker can join an improvement group which is using that method to address a real problem in the plant. The procedure helps employees to master the procedures quickly and greatly increases the effectiveness of the courses.

Training must be recurrent and delivered in a series of short sessions lasting a few hours per week. In general, 5–10 per cent of a line worker's time should be spent in learning new methods and applying new improvement skills on the job. Managers can emphasize the results by insisting that subordinates use the key concepts stressed in training. For example, if people are being trained to use cause-and-effect and Pareto charts, these tools should be employed in reports and meetings on related subjects. Visual aids can also be used to indicate which methods are presently being used in the improvement programme. These precautions reenforce the impact of training courses and make it less likely that supervisors and workers will revert to old practices when under stress.

Manufacturers in developing countries frequently offer additional courses in basic education to raise literacy and numeracy levels. These programmes are conducted in the employee's own time but have successfully increased literacy and boosted workers' commitment to the firm (Wilson, 1992).

Along with various training courses, the transition to continuous improvement will usually require significant modifications in a company's system of incentives. Direct competition between firms in the marketplace yields substantial benefits to consumers, but competition among individuals in the same firm can be detrimental to improvement efforts. Incentive structures that create barriers to cooperation and information exchange between staff undermine the firm's ability to respond quickly to changes in the competitive environment. A concurrence of incentives is necessary, with all members of the firm working towards the common goal of customer satisfaction.

Numerical targets are one form of incentives that may inhibit improvement efforts. 'Zero defects' and specific targets for sales or cost-cutting programmes are common examples of numerical goals. One drawback is that targets usually refer to specific divisions or groups in a firm and may conflict with goals set for other parts of the same organization. Another common flaw is that workers are rarely provided with any guidance as to how to realize these goals.[12] Finally, numerical targets divert attention from the more fundamental issue of statistical variation. If manufacturing processes are statistically stable, numerical goals serve little purpose. Those that exceed a firm's capability can not be reached, despite the best efforts of workers. Conversely, if manufacturing processes are unstable, managers have no way of knowing what their system can produce and numerical goals become meaningless. Without sufficient knowledge of their production system, managers may even misinterpret random variation as proof of the success or failure of improvement efforts.

Similar comments apply to incentives involving work standards, piece-work and incentive pay. Work standards are based on an average worker's rate of production and are used to predict or control costs. Peer pressure discourages the more productive workers from surpassing the established work standard or quota, while those who are less productive can not achieve that rate. Job dissatisfaction, employee turnover, more defects and a greater amount of rework are typical consequences. Reliance on incentive pay and piece-work forms of payment can be equally ineffective. Workers soon realize that they will be paid even if many of the items they produce are defective. Some managers try to discourage this practice by refusing to pay for defective items. But without a knowledge of their manufacturing processes, they can not determine whether the problem is due to a worker's poor performance or to flaws in the production system. Inspectors and workers may not agree on the definition of a defective item, and the criterion can vary from one inspector to the next. Ultimately, each of these incentives methods can jeopardize improvement efforts by effectively setting a ceiling on the rate of progress in a plant (Deming, 1982).

The search for more effective types of incentive measures can begin by recognizing several basic principles. First, managers should make it clear that everyone's job is to increase customer satisfaction by steadily improving the production system. Second, they must ensure that all workers understand their individual roles and are prepared to perform their duties. Once these points are clarified, supervisors can begin to collect data on performance. However, everyone should understand that this exercise is part of the overall improvement effort and is not intended to single out any individual for punishment (see Box 7.5).

A similar line of reasoning applies when attention turns to more general types of incentives linking manufacturers with their suppliers. During the 1970s and 1980s, many mass producers thought they could meet the challenges of Japanese CIFs by slashing production costs and maintaining low prices. Purchasing managers were urged to seek out the cheapest suppliers and most buyer–seller relationships were only as good as the next quote. This practice exacerbated quality problems and inhibited the development of competitive abilities. Meanwhile, CIFs gained market share through process improvements and long-term relationships with high-quality suppliers.

Firms soon realized that awarding contracts purely on the basis of price was not an effective type of incentive measure. The savings gained by pitting one supplier against another are later lost due to the costs of questionable quality. More rework, supplier returns, larger stocks and various other hidden costs make the practice of accepting the lowest bid a losing proposition. Rather than viewing suppliers as bargaining adversaries, firms must reorder their incentive

---

**Box 7.5   Monitoring workers' performance**

Managers can begin to collect data on workers' performance once it is clear that their motive is to improve production processes and workers' performance. A series of weekly samples can be collected for various work assignments in the factory. The results can be compared against relevant characteristics such as experience and levels of training. Those who are good candidates for advanced training can be identified, while those needing special assistance can be helped or placed in a different job. Workers should soon realize that managers are supporting them rather than attempting to penalize them for a poor performance.

systems to allow them to reap the advantages of long-term buyer–supplier partnerships (Ray, 1992).

Manufacturers may also need to take the lead in persuading governments to introduce some of the measures we have described above. Industrialists and engineers in developing countries are far more knowledgeable about the methods of continuous improvement than are public officials. They can exert pressure on governments to provide high-level support in this field. By collaborating with each other and working through industrial associations and chambers of commerce, firms can influence spending on education, training, metrology, standards and other parts of a nation-wide programme. Rather than lobbying for protection and other concessions from the government, small and medium-sized manufacturers might seek support in the form of subsidies or tax breaks for training and materials for continuous improvement. Government should be pressured to make the widespread use of continuous improvement a top priority.

In conclusion, we have championed the cause of continuous improvement throughout this book and firmly believe the methods are an essential ingredient for successful industrialization in many developing countries. The true advantage of these procedures lies not in the ability to raise quality or reduce costs. These achievements are important but are not ends in themselves. The ultimate goal is more ambitious: to give firms the capability and flexibility to respond effectively to a variety of customers' demands while still realizing higher levels of productivity.

This broad goal brings us back to some of the themes set out in the first chapter of this book. Today's increasingly turbulent environment places a premium on a firm's flexibility and the capacity to adapt. Such attributes were less important in the earlier era when manufacturers could carve out a market niche and then take precautions to defend their position. The change has been a significant one for firms in industrialized countries, but for those in developing countries it is traumatic. Markets in the latter countries have long been fragmented and populated with obedient customers, captive and dependent suppliers and slack competitors. But this reality is rapidly changing as privatization, foreign investment and freer trade lead to greater integration of the world's economies. Firms in developing countries must rapidly upgrade their managerial skills and their governments must help. There is a danger that they will be sidetracked by opting for one or more of the faddish themes that pass through the managerial literature every year. Continuous improvement, however, is a proven method with a long period of gestation and a history of success. It offers an excellent starting point from which to build a successful cadre of managers for the twenty-first century.

# NOTES

1. A limited amount of evidence is available for firms implementing programmes of total quality management and total quality control. For example, surveys carried out in the United Kingdom and the United States suggest that only 20–40 per cent of the companies believe their quality programmes have achieved tangible results. Some of the techniques employed by these firms are also used by followers of continuous improvement. However, the quality programmes generally have more complicated and ambitious objectives and their rates of success should be lower than for continuous improvement.
2. There are many models for assessing the 'cost of quality' (such as those of Juran or Taguchi). However, attempting to quantify in dollar terms the gains from the continuous improvement of processes, products, services and training is problematic — indeed the manager about to embark on a programme of continuous improvement should know that he can only quantify a small part of the gains (Deming, 1986, pp. 121–3).
3. The wave of layoffs occurring in the early 1990s was not driven by improvement programmes, though many firms used the tools of continuous improvement to expedite the process of streamlining their workforce. For instance, half the participants in a study of Fortune 1000 companies acknowledged that the outcome of these programmes was to eliminate several layers of management and supervision (Lawler, et al., 1992).
4. This section draws heavily on the work of A. Bós and the authors gratefully acknowledge his contribution to this book.
5. While the cultural influences upon managerial style are less critical than organizational structures, there can be problems if a manager does not share the same cultural background with subordinates. For example, a paternalistic Nigerian manager may increase improvements on the shop floor in a plant in Nigeria. However, this same manager — although technically competent — may encounter difficulties using the same approach in another culture. Japanese managers have encountered difficulties of this type when introducing methods of continuous improvement in plants outside Japan.
6. The Swiss and German examples of three-year apprenticeships point to the benefits derived by both students and industry from such training and collaboration.
7. For example, UNIDO staff interviewed over 250 plant managers, engineers and technicians in developing countries. All these individuals were employed in subsidiaries of some of the world's largest multinationals and the majority of local staff they hired were trained in nearby institutions. Curiously, none of the interviews revealed any systematic contacts between the staff of multinationals and local educational institutions. No instances of collaboration or classroom presentations were noted.
8. There may be resistance on the part of faculty to perceived interloping by non-academics.
9. A permanent centre need not be located at a university. A stand-alone centre can also be established with assistance from private industry.
10. In most Japanese CIFs, such training is required for promotion at each step in the organization.
11. Examples are the statistical design of experiments and parameter design using Taguchi methods.
12. Numerical targets which are put in place without supplying the necessary training and tools will only create low morale and discredit improvement programmes. Workers are likely to get the impression that management has no plan other than urging employees to work harder. On the other hand, if managers make it clear that they are pursuing a concrete plan to improve the system, and if they ensure that workers are trained and understand exactly what is expected, then morale should increase. Management must channel the brains and experience of employees into an effort to change the system so everyone can worker smarter — not harder.

# SUGGESTED READING

## I.  General Reading on the Tools and Management of Continuous Improvement

Asian Productivity Organization (1972), *Japan Quality Control Circles*, Tokyo: Asian Productivity Organization.

Bhote, Keki R. (1987), *Supplier Management*, New York: American Management Association.

Deming, W. Edwards (1986), *Out of the Crisis*, Cambridge, MA: MIT Center for Advanced Engineering Study.

Ernst and Young Quality and Improvement Consulting Group (1992), *Total Quality: A Manager's Guide for the 1990s*, London: Kogan Page Limited.

Hall, Robert W. *(1897), Attaining Manufacturing Excellence*, Homewood, IL: Dow-Jones-Irwin.

Imai, Masaaki (1985), *What is Total Quality Control?: The Japanese Way*, Englewood Cliffs, NJ: Prentice-Hall.

_____ (1986), *Kaizen: The Key to Japan's Manufacturing Success*, New York: Random House.

Juran, Joseph M. (1989), *Juran on Leadership for Quality*, New York: Free Press.

Mizuno, Shigeru (1988), *Company-Wide Total Quality Control*, Tokyo: Asian Productivity Organization.

Porter, Michael E. (1985), *Competitive Advantage: Creating and Sustaining Superior Performance*, New York: Free Press.

Scholtes, Peter R. (1988), *The Team Handbook*, Madison, WI: Joiner Associates.

Schonberger, Richard J. (1986), *World Class Manufacturing: The Lessons of Simplicity Applied*, New York: Free Press.

Shingo, Shigeo (1985), *A Revolution in Manufacturing: The SMED System*, Stamford, CT: Productivity Inc.

Stahl, M. and G. Bounds (eds) (1991), *Competing Globally Through Customer Value*, New York: Quorum Books.

Takahashi, Y. and T. Osada, (1990), *TPM: Total Productive Maintenance*, Tokyo: Asian Productivity Organization.

Thomas, Brain (1992), *Total Quality Training: The Quality Culture and the Quality Trainer*, Berkshire: McGraw-Hill Book Company Europe.

## II.  Statistical Methods of Quality Control

Deming, W. Edwards (1982), *Quality, Productivity, and Competitive Position*, Cambridge, MA: MIT Center for Advanced Engineering Study.

Ishikawa, Kaoru (1982), *Guide to Quality Control*, Tokyo: Asian Productivity Organization.

Kume, Hitoshi (1985), *Statistical Methods for Quality Improvement*, Tokyo: AOTS.

Taguchi, Genichi (1986), *Introduction to Quality Engineering*, Tokyo: Asian Productivity Organization.

Wadsworth, H., K. Stephens and A. Godfrey (1986), *Modern Methods for Quality Control and Improvement*, New York: John Wiley & Sons.

### III.  Background and Global Implications of Continuous Improvement

Best, Michael H. (1990), *The New Competition: Institutions of Industrial Restructuring*, Cambridge, MA: Harvard University Press.

Cole, William E. and John W. Mogab (1994), *The Economics of Total Quality Management: Clashing Paradigms in the Global Economy*, Cambridge, MA: Blackwell Press.

# Appendix: A Closer Look at the Statistical Tools

The practice of compiling monthly indicators to monitor business performance is well known and widely accepted. Measures will vary from one industry to another but familiar examples include: output per worker hour, costs of purchased materials per unit of output, value of goods in inventory and time lost through accidents or breakdowns. Quantitative indicators such as these can serve many purposes. They may be used to compare current performance with previous trends, determine positive or negative trends in overall business activity, performance and efficiency, compare the performance at different sites operated by the firm and so on.

Managers working with these measures know they will vary over time. They are also aware of strategies and tactics which can be employed to alter the indicators. All too often, this is the limit of the user's appreciation of these matters. One of the main concerns of this book is the depth of the manager's understanding and the range of viable choices he has to alter the outputs and costs being measured. Managers' typical uses of such quantitative information are rather unimaginative. They may compare current results with some forecast or expectation, or evaluate current performance in relation to previous trends. Rarely do they go any further. Such an orientation significantly restricts the benefits to be derived from the data.

A much more fruitful approach is to use all the information available in an effort to determine why indicators behave as they do. By treating current evidence as part of a longer series of results, and by making judgements in the light of the variations observed, managers are able to evaluate current and past practice and to assess the reliability of their forecasts. The distinction between common and special causes of variation represents a first step in this direction. The two concepts are meant to serve as guidelines to identify and eliminate erratic variability, whenever it occurs.

Aside from recognizing different sources of variation, the manager requires a deeper understanding of the idea of variation. Frequently, the monthly indicator's deviation from some standard is treated as just another isolated disruption in the manufacturing system. When this line of reasoning prevails, common and special causes become mingled. The arguments in this book are predicated on a different view: the majority of deviations are a direct consequence of the production system or way of doing things. In the long term the

system will yield many outcomes as a result of process variation. This
continuum represents the effects of all past decisions and practices and contains
information that can serve as a guide for improvement in the future. Accordingly, managers must track variation over long periods of time in order to learn
about the causes and effects of critical parts of the manufacturing system.

The need for a system-wide perspective to monitor variation follows directly
from the foregoing line of reasoning. Managers with limited information on
variation may readily assume there can be only one reason for the deviations
they observe. By focusing on only that potential source of variation, they ignore
others which may be more important. Even when the manager identifies a
genuine problem, the remedial action can have unintended negative effects
since other reasons for variation are ignored. Our objections to the use of
certain numerical standards are based in part on their incompatibility with a
system-wide approach.

Several of the statistical tools which can be used in a system-wide approach
to continuous improvement were introduced in Chapter 5. This appendix
provides more details and examples of how statistical methods can be used in
a programme of CIT.

## PROCESS FLOW CHARTS

Before beginning to study any manufacturing process, engineers and managers
must clearly understand the interrelationships between that process and other
parts of the production system. Subsequent investigation may reveal several
very different opportunities for improvement and a process flow chart is needed
to determine which of these are consistent with the firm's overall priorities. To
fulfil its intended role, the flow chart must serve three purposes. It should:

- accurately and completely describe the manufacturing process;

- identify the steps or points in the manufacturing process where measurements can be taken; and

- single out all the potential causal factors that need to be considered before
collection of data is begun.

The steps involved in creating a process flow chart were spelled out in the
text. A simplified example of a flow chart referring to the assembly of hornpads
for cars was also presented there (see Figure 5.1). A more complete version of
that same chart is reproduced in Figure A.I. The shaded areas indicate certain
steps which make no contribution to value added (notably, inspection and

*Figure A.I    Revised flow chart of a hornpad assembly process*

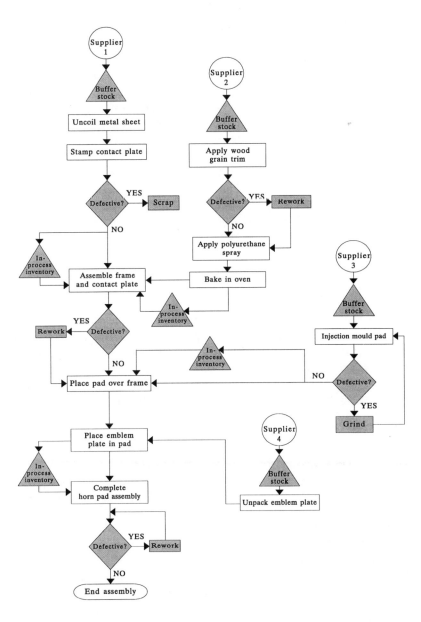

non-value-added activities

*Source*: UNIDO

storage of buffer stock). These operations may be necessary when current levels of statistical variation are high or knowledge of the process is limited, but they are also costly. The reliability of the assembly process could be greatly improved if variation is reduced. Non-essential steps can then be curtailed and eventually eliminated.

Many manufacturing processes require flow charts of considerable complexity. Because these are difficult to read, they are sometimes replaced with a 'top-down' version showing process steps across the top of the page with more detailed information listed below. Figure A.II provides an example of one of these top-down charts taken from a study of the bottlenecks encountered when cooling chocolate syrup to the correct temperature before filling containers.

In summary, process flow charts are an important preliminary step in a larger statistical exercise. Charts which merely list the order in which operations should occur will not adequately serve the purposes set out here. Once a detailed and accurate version has been developed, collection of data can begin and attention turns to some of the other statistical tools described in Chapter 5.

## CAUSE-AND-EFFECT DIAGRAMS

Analysts should try to specify problems and their potential causes at an early stage. It is unlikely that a complete list of the causes and effects can be developed prior to collection of data. A preliminary cause-and-effect analysis will nevertheless increase the chances of successfully identifying sources of problems. We illustrate the application of this tool with the help of an example, describing the development of both the process flow chart and a preliminary cause-and-effect diagram.

The plant studied here produces individual servings of frozen meat pies (known as pot pies) in metal trays. Standard practice was to inspect every bottom crust produced and to remove any which had breaks in the dough or did not completely cover the bottom of the metal tray. Statistical evaluation showed that the system was in control. Nevertheless, a large number of crusts (18 per cent) had to be scrapped after they were placed in the metal trays but before the filling had been added.

The management group charged with introducing improvements could not agree that the large proportion of nonconforming crusts represented a 'quality' problem. Some argued that there was no problem since every crust was inspected and defective ones were removed from the production line. Nor did they believe there was any waste because the discarded dough was reused at a later stage in the process. Other members of the group disagreed, arguing that the machine and operator time used to produce items which could not be sold was an unnecessary expense. They also believed that the taste and texture of

*Figure A.II  Example of a top-down flow chart*

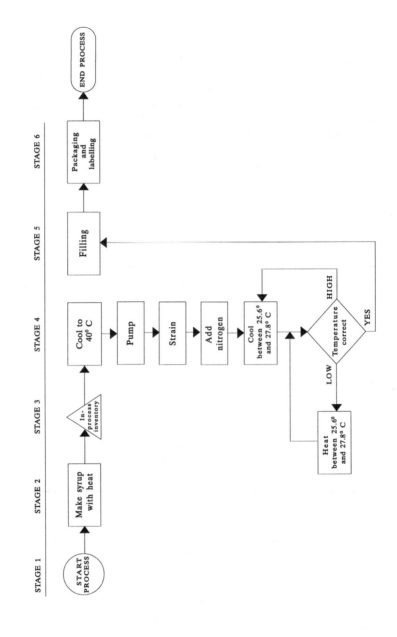

*161*

the crust deteriorated if the dough was reworked, making this procedure an inappropriate solution.

Eventually, the management group decided that more information was needed and the process flow chart shown in Figure A.III was constructed. Discussion of this diagram led to no agreement on the source of any problems. The next step in the investigation was for two members of the management group to meet with operators of the production line and develop a cause-and-effect diagram. This analysis is reproduced in Figure A.IV. Some members of the group hypothesized that the proportion of defective crusts may be higher on certain days or at certain times of the day. No decision could be made about the two suspicions of the group. Still more information was needed before this

*Figure A.III    Sample of a process flow diagram*

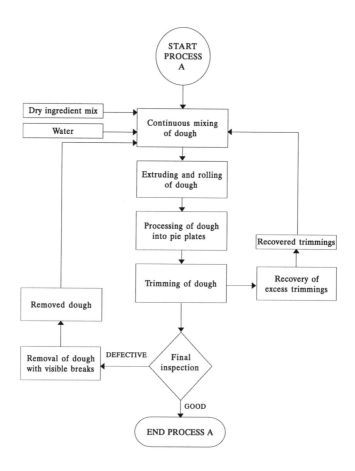

*Figure A.IV   Cause-and-effect diagram*

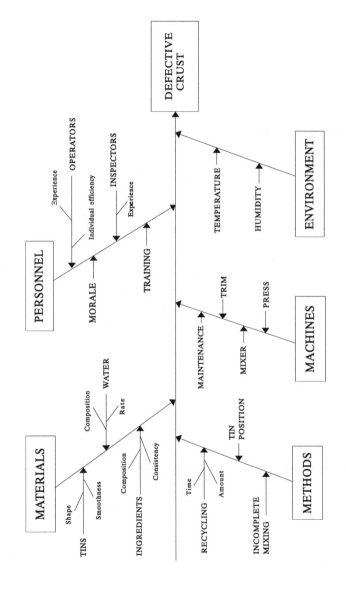

hypothesis could be tested. The group agreed that a control chart would be needed to monitor the results of the production process. We return to this example later in the appendix when that tool is discussed.

## PARETO DIAGRAMS

In the situation described above there was considerable uncertainty about likely sources of variation and some doubt that variation was excessive. The circumstances will be more obvious in many cases, and when they are, managers will want to know which of the acknowledged sources of variation are the most troublesome. Construction of a Pareto diagram will help to answer their questions. The basis for this analysis is that a few categories or sources of variation will typically cause a disproportionate number of all problems. Analysts must first decide how to categorize defects and then count the number of events in each category. Data might be arranged according to defects by type, accidents by type, impurities by type or in some similar fashion.

One version of a Pareto diagram referring to the assembly of hornpads for steering wheels was described in the text. That exercise revealed that nearly 74 per cent of all defects could be attributed to three different categories of flaws (see Figure 5.4). After further study, engineers determined that two of these categories, surface defects and excessive flash, could only occur during the moulding process. The third involved improper assembly, missing parts and loose nuts and was traced to the assembly process. On the basis of this information, a new set of categories was created which identified defects according to their point of origin in the manufacturing process. The results of that exercise are reproduced in Figure A.V. The pad-moulding process accounts for the largest share of defects and should be the most fruitful place to look for improvements.

Pareto diagrams supply valuable information but they must be interpreted carefully. The two most common dangers are:

- the failure to recognize that the number of occurrences in each category are themselves subject to variation;

- the danger of drawing improper conclusions about the relationships between causes and effects on the basis of the diagram.

Unexpected shifts in variance are likely if only a limited amount of information has been collected. For example, data referring to the results of one week's operations could suggest a degree of variability quite different from that based on several weeks of observation. An accurate estimate requires that data be compiled over multiple time periods. Only then is the analyst able to

*Figure A.V    Pareto diagram showing defects by process step*

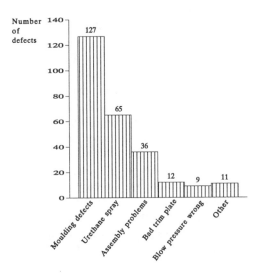

distinguish between problems which are severe and those which are only transient.

The second difficulty cited here can be best illustrated by an example. The manufacturer in this case produces an assembly designed to spray a liquid into a chamber. Leakage from the assembly was seen as the critical defect. After inspecting several leaking assemblies, the source of the problem was thought to be a particular component that was contaminated by foreign matter. Workers assumed that contamination was the source of leakage and the supplier of the component prepared to add a costly step to decontaminate its production process.

Fortunately, some non-leaking assemblies produced during the same period of time were belatedly examined. These were found to have the same type and degree of contamination as the leaking assemblies. Since contamination existed in both sets, there had to be other reasons for the leakages. Further investigation showed that excessive variation in component dimensions was the real source of the problem. This unexpected result underlines the need for investigators to study both defective and problem-free items before reaching any conclusion about the source of variation.

## HISTOGRAMS

As the collection of data proceeds, investigators learn more about the manufacturing system and its various processes. This allows them to gain a much greater understanding of the operation but it also means that the volume of data to be handled becomes extremely large. Construction of a histogram allows the user to see the overall pattern of occurrences at a glance. The mound- or bell-shaped histogram described in Chapter 5 is common, but other patterns will also be encountered. Regardless of their shape, each histogram should be explainable in terms of the characteristics being measured, the process of measurement itself, or other features of the manufacturing system.

Figure A.VI offers several examples. Histogram a) describes a 'comb-shaped' pattern where the occurrence of events rises and falls from one category to the next. An abnormal shape such as this may be due to instrument measurement errors, rounding errors in the data or other inconsistencies. Histogram b displays a 'cliff-shaped' pattern with a sharp drop in occurrences at one end of the graph. This result is frequently observed by purchasers of

*Figure A.VI    Common patterns for histograms*

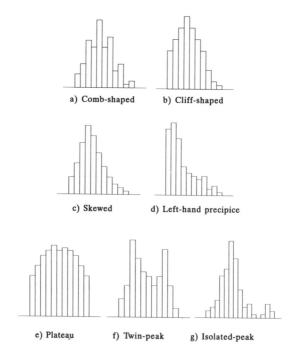

a) Comb-shaped      b) Cliff-shaped

c) Skewed      d) Left-hand precipice

e) Plateau      f) Twin-peak      g) Isolated-peak

materials or parts. Typically, the vendor will not ship items that fail to meet a certain standard (presumably because they fall below buyers' specifications). In this case it will be necessary for the buyer to inspect all incoming parts from the vendor. The vendor should also be advised to improve his product quality, not by inspection, but by process improvement. Histograms may also be skewed to the right or left of the centre as in c). In contrast to the normal distribution, the frequency of observations falls off abruptly on one side of the distribution. Such a pattern can result from the imposition of a lower or upper limit; most items which do not meet this standard will be excluded before the inspection process. Histograms in these forms indicate the need for closer investigation of the manufacturing process.

Other patterns resemble a precipice, a plateau, a bi-modal or twin-peaked histogram and an isolated peak. Each may have a different cause. A precipice-like pattern can occur when all items are subjected to inspection due to high variation. A plateau-shaped version results when several distributions having different mean values are mixed together. Bi-modal or twin-peak histograms can occur when two distributions with widely different mean values are inadvertently mixed together. Finally, a histogram with an isolated peak could indicate there is some abnormality in the manufacturing process, that there are measurement errors or that data from a different process has been included.

Whatever their shape, histograms are a useful way to relate a sample distribution to pre-determined boundaries or specifications. Some examples can be found in Figure A.VII. In panel a) the distribution of the sample falls within the upper ($S_U$) and lower ($S_L$) limits. This result suggests that the process

*Figure A.VII   Histograms with specification limits*

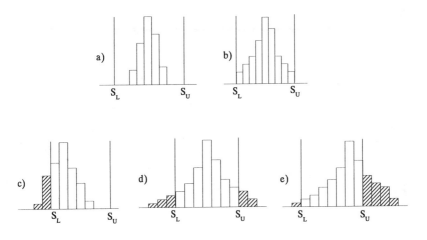

operates well within specifications, although ongoing improvement is always desirable. In panel b), specifications are barely satisfied and efforts to reduce variation are needed. Other histograms show that specifications are not being met and some remedial action is clearly needed to reduce variation. In such cases flow diagrams, cause-and-effect charts or control charts supply supplementary information about the source of problems.

# USING CONTROL CHARTS TO MONITOR VARIATION

Control charts are an effective means of extending our knowledge of manufacturing process and production systems. They supply visual evidence of excessive, or out-of-control, variation and indicate instability in the process due to special causes. The charts may also be used to gauge the success of efforts to remove special causes of variation or to decide when system-wide variation demands more detailed study of individual processes.

One of the simplest applications of control charts is the study of product characteristics that can not be measured on a continuous scale. These characteristics, which are more generally known as 'product attributes', are of interest when firms wish to monitor the quality or performance of their products. Managers must first establish clear 'pass-or-fail' definitions which determine the criteria for acceptance. One example of a product attribute would be the number of damaged cans in a sample of 1,000. Another would be the number of shafts in a sample of 200 which fail to meet specifications. Based on simple characterizations such as these, managers can monitor the quality of their products.

## Percentage Control Charts (p charts)

Once sufficient information on product attributes has been compiled, it is used to construct a control chart. Quite often, managers want to know the proportion of defective items. An estimate can be obtained by constructing a percentage control chart or p chart. This figure will show the variation in the proportion of 'failures' over an extended period of time. If the rejection rate proves to be relatively stable, managers are able to predict future levels of variation with some confidence.

A simple application of a p chart was described in Chapter 5 (see Figure 5.8). The purpose of that exercise was to determine whether an engine-assembly operation was in control or not. After defining the pass-or-fail criterion for assembled engines (that is, the product attribute), engineers set up an inspection plan. They agreed that each week's output would represent a production lot and that 100 engines (the subgroup) would be drawn at random from each lot and inspected. This process was repeated for 21 consecutive weeks and the results are reported in Table A.1.

The investigation eventually confirmed that no special sources of variation existed but before this conclusion could be reached, the average number of defectives (also known as the centre line or $\bar{p}$) and the upper and lower control limits all had to be determined. Below, we show the calculations for each of these measures.

The centre line ($\bar{p}$) is defined as

$$\bar{p} = \frac{\text{total number of nonconforming items}}{\text{total number of items inspected}}$$

Based on the data in Table A.1, 131 of the 2,100 engines inspected were found to be defective. Therefore,

$$\bar{p} = \frac{131}{2100} = 0.0624$$

To determine acceptable levels of variation when the process is stable, engineers must calculate the upper and lower control limits. These two values

*Table A.1    Collecting data on product attributes: number of defective engine assemblies per week*

| Inspection week | Number rejected | Percentage of defectives (p values)[a] | Inspection week | Number rejected | Percentage of defectives (p values)[a] |
|---|---|---|---|---|---|
| 1 | 6 | 0.06 | 12 | 5 | 0.05 |
| 2 | 8 | 0.08 | 13 | 7 | 0.07 |
| 3 | 2 | 0.02 | 14 | 8 | 0.08 |
| 4 | 3 | 0.03 | 15 | 11 | 0.11 |
| 5 | 5 | 0.05 | 16 | 3 | 0.03 |
| 6 | 10 | 0.10 | 17 | 5 | 0.05 |
| 7 | 4 | 0.04 | 18 | 9 | 0.09 |
| 8 | 7 | 0.07 | 19 | 5 | 0.05 |
| 9 | 2 | 0.02 | 20 | 7 | 0.07 |
| 10 | 12 | 0.12 | 21 | 2 | 0.02 |
| 11 | 10 | 0.10 | – | – | – |

[a]    The number of engines inspected in each week was 100.

depend on the weekly variation in defects and the average number of defects for the entire test period. The formulas and calculations for these limits are given in equations (1) and (2) below.

(1) $\quad UCL_p = \bar{p} + 3\sqrt{\frac{\bar{p}(1-\bar{p})}{n}} = 0.0624 + 3\sqrt{\frac{0.0624(1-0.0624)}{n}}$

(2) $\quad LCL_p = \bar{p} - 3\sqrt{\frac{\bar{p}(1-\bar{p})}{n}} = 0.0624 - 3\sqrt{\frac{0.0624(1-0.0624)}{n}}$

where $\bar{p}$ is defined as above and n is the subgroup size (100 in this case). Accordingly, the control limits are found to be:

$\quad\quad$ UCL = $\quad$ 0.1350 and
$\quad\quad$ LCL = $-$ 0.0102

The lower control limit yields a meaningless result: there is no such thing as a 'negative fraction' of defectives. Thus we have an upper control limit of 0.1350 (13.5 defectives per 100) and a lower control limit which, in practice, is zero.

Confident that no special causes of variation are at work, engineers can now turn their attention to the genuine work of continuous improvement — for example, the search to reduce and eventually eliminate random-cause variation occurring in the system. These matters take us beyond the scope of this book but we can mention a few lines for subsequent investigation. Likely sources of common-cause variation could be: the capability of the equipment used to manufacture the engines, the maintenance practices for this equipment, the engine's design, alterations to that design and the methods used during production of the engine. Among these sources there are many different circumstances which could give rise to common-cause variation. One possibility is that the metal from which the engine block is cast varies in its degree of hardness. If the variations are substantial, machining operations would require differing amounts of time to complete and not all engines would receive adequate machining. Some would be improperly machined, possibly resulting in oil leakage or inadequate combustion characteristics. Problems such as these might occur at any time during the manufacture of the engine and would therefore be common to all outcomes.

## Control Charts Based on the Count of Events (np charts)

So far, the charts and diagrams described here tell us about statistical stability, but very little about the way operations or steps in the manufacturing process contribute to defects. To see how more information may be obtained, we return to our earlier example of a plant producing frozen meat pies. Construction of a process flow chart and a cause-and-effect diagram failed to provide sufficient evidence to determine whether the proportion of defective crusts might be higher on particular days or at certain times of the day.

An inspection process was begun in order to accumulate enough data to construct a control chart. The mechanics of data collection naturally followed the methods of production. First, the operator in charge of making bottom crusts was asked to count the number of nonconforming crusts produced hourly during the work day for a period of five days. Each machine went through four cycles in an hour, producing 24 crusts in every cycle. Accordingly, the hourly production of 96 crusts was treated as a subgroup. Finally, the production line operated with one shift per day and was run for a seven-hour period, meaning that a total of 35 subgroups were included in the experiment.

Because the size of each subgroup was large (96 crusts per hour), management decided that it would be simpler to plot the *number* of defectives rather than their proportion in total production. This decision distinguishes the control chart developed here from the one in our engine-assembly example. The present version is known as an *np chart* because its characteristics are expressed in terms of the number of defectives and not the proportion in the total.

Table A.2 summarizes the results of the five-day experiment. From this data the centre line ($n\bar{p}$) and the lower and upper control limits can be calculated. The centre line, $n\bar{p}$, is defined to be:

$$n\bar{p} = \frac{\text{total number of nonconforming items}}{\text{number of subgroups}}$$

Based on the data in Table A.2, a total of 579 nonconforming crusts were identified in the 35 subgroups. Therefore:

$$n\bar{p} = \frac{579}{35} = 16.5429$$

Before we can calculate the upper and lower control limits for this chart, the value of $\bar{p}$ (defined as $n\bar{p}$ divided by n) must be determined. Accordingly,

$$\bar{p} = \frac{16.5429}{96} = 0.1723$$

The upper and lower control limits (UCL and LCL respectively), can then be calculated using the following formulas:

*Table A.2   Collecting data for an np chart* [a]

| | Time of inspection | Number of nonconforming items[b] | | Time of inspection | Number of nonconforming items[b] |
|---|---|---|---|---|---|
| Monday | 8:00 a | 15 | Thursday | 8:00 a | 15 |
| | 9:00 a | 16 | | 9:00 a | 16 |
| | 10:00 a | 17 | | 10:00 a | 18 |
| | 11:00 a | 20 | | 11:00 a | 18 |
| | 12:00 a | 12 | | 12:00 a | 16 |
| | 1:00 p | 19 | | 1:00 p | 12 |
| | 2:00 p | 13 | | 2:00 p | 16 |
| Tuesday | 8:00 a | 18 | Friday | 8:00 a | 11 |
| | 9:00 a | 27 | | 9:00 a | 17 |
| | 10:00 a | 16 | | 10:00 a | 11 |
| | 11:00 a | 21 | | 11:00 a | 18 |
| | 12:00 a | 22 | | 12:00 a | 15 |
| | 1:00 p | 20 | | 1:00 p | 14 |
| | 2:00 p | 19 | | 2:00 p | 19 |
| | | | | Total | 579 |
| Wednesday | 8:00 a | 9 | | | |
| | 9:00 a | 14 | | | |
| | 10:00 a | 18 | | | |
| | 11:00 a | 23 | | | |
| | 12:00 a | 19 | | | |
| | 1:00 p | 12 | | | |
| | 2:00 p | 13 | | | |

[a]   For a description of the data collection process, see the text.
[b]   A total of 96 bottom crusts are produced each hour and all are inspected.

$$\text{UCL}_{np} = n\bar{p} + 3\sqrt{n\bar{p}(1-\bar{p})}$$

$$\text{LCL}_{np} = n\bar{p} - 3\sqrt{n\bar{p}(1-\bar{p})}$$

From the data in Table A.2, the two limits are:

$$\text{UCL}_{np} = 16.5429 + 3\sqrt{16.5429\,(1-0.1723)} = 27.6439$$

$$\text{LCL}_{np} = 16.5429 - 3\sqrt{16.5429\,(1 - 0.1723)} = 5.4419$$

These values, together with the 35 observations for the average number of defectives in each hourly subgroup, make up the np chart in Figure A.VIII. The completed chart gives no reason to suspect that special causes of variation are at work. Based on the hourly samples taken throughout the week, the proportion of defective pie crusts proves to be stable — about 17 per cent do not conform to acceptable standards.

At first glance it appears that the firm has gone through a rather lengthy exercise to confirm what was already known: about 18 per cent of all items were judged to be defective. However, additional insights can be culled from the chart regarding areas where improvements can be made. For example, there is no evidence that special causes operate during some hours or days but not in others. Since the production process behaves consistently from hour to hour and day to day, those elements in the cause-and-effect diagram which might give rise to such a problem can be disregarded. Further investigation would have to proceed along other lines and the np chart is helpful in identifying this path. Managers know that no special causes are at work from hour to hour but they can not be sure that systematic problems do not arise during one of the four-hourly cycles. Information on this aspect of the operation is not available because the output of all four cycles were lumped together in one subgroup. To be certain about what is happening during a particular hour of operation, the issue of testing and sampling must be examined in more detail and the interested reader should consult additional sources (see, for example, Wadsworth, et al., 1986).

## ADDITIONAL TESTS FOR PRODUCT ATTRIBUTES

Many product attributes can be expressed in terms of simple, pass-or-fail criteria. When that is the case, the types of control charts described above (p or np charts) are useful. There are other types of product attributes, however, which cannot be expressed in such a straightforward way. Some examples are the number of surface flaws on a sheet of material or the number of defective solderings in a piece of electronic equipment. The count of events occurring over time is another way to characterize product attributes. Here, obvious possibilities would be the number of production-line stops, the number of service calls made or the number of customer complaints received.

Product attributes such as these can not be analysed in terms of the p or np charts described above. Among other alternatives, two of the more common are:

*Figure A.VIII    Monitoring the occurrence of defects: illustration of an np chart*

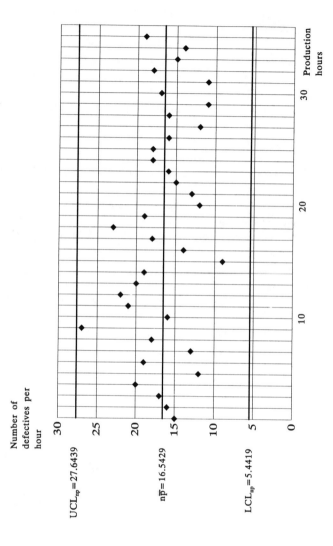

- A 'C chart' which is used to analyse the number of defects in *identical* products or the number occurring in a *fixed period of time*. A practical application would be the study of defects or nonconformities found in uniform sets of products or materials such as sheets of plasterboard, bicycles or boxes of bolts. C charts can also be employed to analyse service performance, for example, the number of incorrect restaurant orders in an eight-hour period.

- A 'U chart' can be employed when the amount of material or the unit of time allowed for inspection *varies* from one subgroup to the next. Examples would include: the inspection of irregular lengths of woven fabric, the number of blemishes on finished furniture or the number of surface defects in differing lengths of brass strips.

The choice of a C or U chart hinges on the *comparability* of the subgroups. If a consistent definition of the subgroup (units inspected, amount of material or identical units of time) can be applied, a C chart is used. When the definition varies from one subgroup to the next, a U chart is chosen. Several other conditions must also be met if either form of control chart is to be appropriate. They include:

- Counts of events must be independent of each other. In other words, the occurrence of events in one subgroup should have no bearing on the number noted in the successive subgroup.

- The number of possible occurrences should be large.

- The probability of an occurrence at any one time or place must be small.

- The expected number of occurrences must be proportional to the amount of time or material which is included in an inspection unit.

These criteria depend on various statistical considerations which are not discussed in this book. However, the reader may get a feel for the requirements from the examples cited above and the discussion which follows.

**Application of a C Chart**

The study of flaws in materials provides an illustration which meets all of the criteria noted above. In this case the material is aluminium sheeting used to manufacture cans. The producer of these cans buys rolls of aluminium sheet from an outside vendor. Some sheets have very small 'pin holes', a defect which results in wasted production time, product and aluminium. In order to learn more about these defects, the manufacturer singled out ten rolls of identical size from one of the supplier's shipments for inspection. The same exercise was repeated 20 times. In all, 20 subgroups consisting of ten rolls were examined for defects. Each subgroup was identical in size and composition, meaning that a C chart is the appropriate choice for studying variation.

Results of the 20 inspections are reported in Table A.3. From this we see that 460 pinholes were discovered during the test period. The average number of defects per inspection unit is determined as follows:

$$\bar{c} = \frac{\text{total number of nonconformities}}{\text{total number of units inspected}}$$

$$\bar{c} = \frac{460}{20} = 23$$

Lower and upper control limits define the amount of variation expected if the process is subject only to random or common causes. The general formulas used to calculate these two limits are, respectively:

$$UCL_c = \bar{c} + 3\sqrt{\bar{c}}$$

$$LCL_c = \bar{c} - 3\sqrt{\bar{c}}$$

*Table A.3    Inspection results for derivation of a C chart*

| Subgroup | Number of holes | Subgroup | Number of holes |
|---|---|---|---|
| 1 | 22 | 11 | 15 |
| 2 | 29 | 12 | 10 |
| 3 | 25 | 13 | 33 |
| 4 | 17 | 14 | 23 |
| 5 | 20 | 15 | 27 |
| 6 | 16 | 16 | 17 |
| 7 | 34 | 17 | 33 |
| 8 | 11 | 18 | 19 |
| 9 | 31 | 19 | 22 |
| 10 | 29 | 20 | 27 |
| | | Total: | 460 |

Inserting the value of $\bar{c}$, the upper control limit is:

$$UCL_c = 23 + 3\sqrt{23} = 37.39$$

Calculations for the lower control limit are:

$$LCL_c = 23 - 3\sqrt{23} = 8.61$$

A completed version of the C chart is reproduced in Figure A.IX. Inspection confirms that all observations are within the control limits and that there is no reason to suspect special causes are at work.

Without improvements by the supplier, the average of 23 holes for every ten rolls of aluminium provides a rough estimate of future defects. Not surprisingly, the manufacturer found this rate to be unacceptably high. The supplier, however, claimed that an investigation carried out at its own plant revealed a much smaller number of defects per roll. Subsequent discussion showed that the supplier's inspections were conducted before rolling, whereas those undertaken by the manufacturer naturally took place after the aluminium had been rolled. Holes could be formed when the supplier makes the aluminium sheets or they may occur during the process of rolling, unrolling, packing or shipping. It was agreed that the supplier would randomly select ten rolls per shipment, record the number of holes and tag each inspected roll. Upon receipt, the manufacturer would unroll the aluminium and count the holes. Based on the results of this experiment, both parties could use flow charts and cause-and-effect charts to determine which steps are the main source of defects.

### Monitoring Variation with a U Chart

If the amount of material or the unit of time varies from one inspection to the next, a U chart is the appropriate monitoring tool. To illustrate the construction, we employ a set of data referring to the number of blemishes found on wooden table tops. Managers and engineers compiled this data by inspecting 20 table tops of varying sizes. The distinguishing characteristic of the U Chart, which is reproduced in Figure A.X, is that the values of control limits will change according to the size of the subgroup. As in our earlier example, there is no lower control limit: a negative number of defects would obviously have no meaning. Since none of the plotted points fall outside the upper limit, we can conclude that the process is in statistical control (for further discussion, see Ishikawa, 1990, pp. 82–3).

*Figure A.IX   Monitoring defects in aluminium sheeting: an application of a C chart*

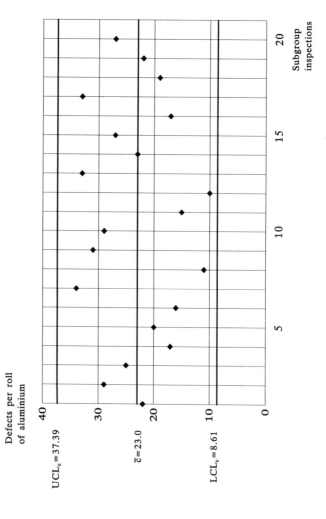

*Figure A.X   Monitoring the occurrence of blemishes: application of a U chart*

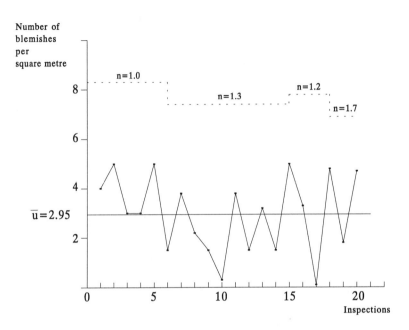

## READING CONTROL CHARTS

Control charts are intended to provide an accurate picture of variation within a process. If anything abnormal is observed, corrective action must be taken. Thus far we have examined processes that were in control, or subject only to common causes of variation. In the real world there will be many instances when a process is out of control. The most obvious cases arise when one or more points fall outside the control limits. However, there are other circumstances or patterns which indicate that a process is out of control. Several of these are discussed below and are illustrated in Figure A.XI (see also Kume, 1992, pp. 107–9 and Ishikawa, 1990, pp. 74–6).

First, a process is regarded as out of control when a 'run', or series of successive observations all fall on one side of the centre line. The number of points included is known as the 'length of the run' and the following runs would indicate that a process is out of control:

- A run of seven or more consecutive points (known as the 'Run of Seven') which falls on the same side of the average indicates abnormality. A

*Figure A.XI    Identifying common patterns and trends in control charts*

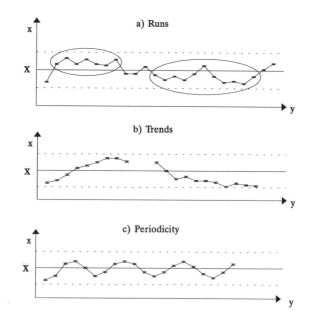

process can also be out of control when: (i) at least ten of eleven consecutive points fall on one side of the centre line; (ii) at least 12 of 14 consecutive points are on one side of the centre line; or (iii) at least 16 of 20 consecutive points meet this criterion.

Patterns which exhibit a clear trend, or some form of periodicity are other signals that a process is out of control. They include:

- Trends in observations which are depicted by a continued rise or fall in a series of observations. Should a series of consecutive observations form a continuous curve (either rising or falling), an abnormality in the manu- facturing process is assumed. Often, such a trend will exceed the control limits before reaching seven points.

- Periodicity which occurs when a repeating up-and-down cycle is observed over similar intervals. Unlike runs and trends, there is no simple way to evaluate this sort of pattern. The best strategy is to track the movement of data points over time. If such a pattern recurs on a regular basis, there is solid evidence of periodicity.

Further evidence that special causes of variation exist can be found when observations are clustered around the control limits or centre line. These 'hugging patterns' often result from an inappropriate arrangement of observations into subgroups, possibly when different types of data have been mixed together in the same subgroups. It may be necessary to change the method of subgrouping, reorganize the data and construct a new control chart.

Two types of hugging patterns are shown in Figure A.XII. One version occurs when observations are narrowly clustered around the centre line or average. To determine if data is 'hugging a centre line', two additional boundaries or limits are needed. These are represented by the dotted lines located halfway between the centre line and the upper and lower control limits. If most or all the observations lie within these two lines, an abnormality exists and the process is assumed to be out of control.

A similar procedure is followed if the investigator suspects that data tends to 'hug the control limits'. In that case, interim boundaries are placed two-thirds of the distance from the centre line to control limits. The process is regarded as out of control if 2 out of 3 points, 3 out of 7, or 4 of 10 points lie outside these boundaries (even though the points may still be within the control limits).

*Figure A.XII    Clustering patterns in control chart data*

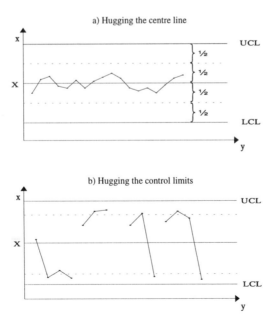

In conclusion, statistical analysis and charting is particularly important in the early stages of continuous improvement, though like all other parts of the programme, they must be tailored to suit the needs of each firm. While workers and technicians are responsible for collecting data and using control charts and other tools used in statistical investigations it is critical that managers support — and understand — such efforts. To be effective, the manager will need some understanding of the purposes and objectives which lie behind the statistician's calculations. We have considered but a few of the methods which would be employed in a programme of SPC. Many important elements have been ignored in the interest of simplicity. Hopefully, the discussion is sufficient to give the reader an impression of how these tools fit into a larger programme of continuous improvement. For a more comprehensive but still elementary treatment of SPC, the reader should consult other sources such as Kume, 1985 and Ishikawa, 1990.

# References

Abegglen, J. and G. Stalk (1985), *Kaisha: The Japanese Corporation*, New York: Basic Books.

Aguayo, R. (1990), *Dr. Deming: The American Who Taught the Japanese about Quality*, New York: Lyle Stuart.

Best, M.H. (1990), *The New Competition: Institutions of Industrial Restructuring*, Cambridge, MA: Harvard University Press.

Bicking, C.A. and F.M. Gryna, Jr. (1974), 'Process Control by Statistical Methods', in *Quality Control Handbook*, New York: McGraw-Hill, Inc.

Bós, A.M.G. (1991), 'Management systems as technology and their relation with development: A comparison of Japanese, U.S. and national firms in Brazil', Unpublished doctoral dissertation, The University of Tennessee, Knoxville.

Bós, A.M.G. (1993), 'Paternalism and Continuous Improvement: A Case Study of the Brazilian Electronics Sector', Working paper, Tusculum University, Tennessee.

Bradley, K. and S. Hill (1987), 'Quality Circles and Managerial Interests' *Industrial Relations*, **21**, pp. 291–311.

Brannon, J.T., D.D. James and G.W. Lucker (1990), 'Promoting Backward Linkages from Assembly Plants in Northern Mexico: An Exercise in Applied Institutional Economics', Paper presented at the annual meeting of the Association for Evolutionary Economics, December.

Chandler, A.D. (1977), *The Visible Hand*, Cambridge, MA: Harvard University Press.

Cole, W.E. (1992), 'Mixed Competition: An Analytical View of the Continuous Improvement Firm Operating in Western Economies', Paper presented at the annual meeting of the North American Economics and Finance Association, New Orleans, January.

Cole, W.E. and J. Mogab (1994), *The Economics of Total Quality Management: Clashing Paradigms in the Global Economy*, Cambridge, MA: Blackwell.

Cole, W.E., J. Mogab and R.D. Sanders (1992), 'Mixed Competition: An Analytical View of the Continuous Improvement Firm Operating in Western Economies', Paper presented at the annual meeting of the North American Economics and Finance Association, New Orleans, January.

Cole, W.E. and R.D. Sanders (1985), 'Internal Migration and Urban Employment in the Third World', *American Economic Review*, **75**, (3), pp. 481–94.

Colman, D. and F. Nixson (1985), *Economies of Change in Less Developed Countries*, Oxford: Philip Allan Publishers.

Deming, W. Edwards (1982), *Quality, Productivity and Competitive Position*, Cambridge, MA: MIT.

Deming, W. Edwards (1986), *Out of the Crisis*, Cambridge, MA: MIT.

Drummond, H. (1992), *The Quality Movement: What Total Quality Management Is Really All About*, London: Nichols Publishing Company.

Fleury, A. and J. Humphrey (1992), 'Recursos Humanos e a Difusão e Adaptacão de Novos Métodos de Qualidade no Brasil', Working paper, Brasília, IPEA

Fleury, M.T.L. (1993), 'The Culture of Quality and the Management of Human Resources', *IDS Bulletin*, **24**, (2), pp. 34–41.

Florida, R. and M. Kenney (1990), *The Breakthrough Illusion: Corporate America's Failure to Move From Mass Production to Innovation*, New York: Basic Books.

Fortuna, R.M. (1992), 'The Quality Imperative', in Ernst and Young Quality and Improvement Consulting Group, *Total Quality: A Manager's Guide for the 1990's*, London: Kogan Page Limited.

Franzoi, N. and M.B. Rodrigues (1993), 'Beyond Quality', *IDS Bulletin*, **24**, (2), pp. 53–7.

Fucini, J. and S. Fucini (1990), *Working for the Japanese: Inside Mazda's American Auto Plant*, New York: The Free Press.

Hayes, R.H. and G.P. Pisano (1994), 'Beyond World-Class: The New Manufacturing Strategy', *Harvard Business Review*, (January–February), pp. 77–86.

Hayes, R.H., S.C. Wheelwright and K.B. Clark (1988), *Dynamic Manufacturing*, New York: The Free Press.

Hibbard, M. and C.J. Hosticka (1982), 'Socially Appropriate Technology: Philosophy in Action', *Humboldt Journal of Social Relations*, **9**, (2), pp. 1–10.

Hill, S. (1991), 'Why Quality Circles Failed but Total Quality Management Might Succeed', *British Journal of Industrial Relations*, **29**, (4).

Hoffman, K. and R. Kaplinsky (1992), 'Transnational Corporations and the Transfer of New Management Practices to Developing Countries', Report prepared for the United National Centre on Transnational Corporations, October.

Hounshell, D.A. (1984), *From the American System to Mass Production, 1800–1932*, Baltimore, MD: Johns Hopkins University Press.

Huge, E.C. (1992), 'Quality of Conformance to Design', in Ernst and Young Quality and Improvement Consulting Group, *Total Quality: A Manager's Guide for the 1990's*, London: Kogan Page Limited.

Imai, M. (1986), *Kaizen*, New York: Random House.

Ishikawa, K. (1990), *Guide to Quality Control*, White Plains, New York: Quality Resources.

Jaikumar, R. (1986), 'Postindustrial Manufacturing', *Harvard Business Review*, **64**, (6), pp. 69–76.

James, D.D. (1974), *Used Machinery and Economic Development*, East Lansing: Michigan State University, International Business and Economic Studies.

Johnson, H.T. and R.S. Kaplan (1987), *The Rise and Fall of Management Accounting*, Boston, MA: Harvard Business School Press.

Julius, D. (1990), *Global Companies and Public Policy: The Growing Challenge of Foreign Direct Investment*, Royal Institute of International Affairs London: Pinter Publishers.

Juran, J. (1988), *Juran on Planning for Quality*, New York: The Free Press.

Juran, J.M. and H.M. Cook, Jr. (1974), 'Inspection and Test', *Quality Control Handbook*, New York: McGraw-Hill, Inc.

Kaplan, R.S. (ed.) (1990), *Measures for Manufacturing Excellence*, Boston: Harvard Business School Press.

Kaplinsky, R. (1993), 'The Diffusion of Organizational Reform in Developing Countries: A Case Study from India', *IDS Bulletin*, **24**, (2), pp. 19–26.

Koura, K. (1972), 'The QC Circle and Human Relations', *Japan Quality Control Circles*, Tokyo: Asian Productivity Organization.

Kume, H. (1985), *Statistical Methods for Quality Improvement*, Tokyo: A.O.T.S.

Kuttner, R. (1993), 'Talking Marriage and Thinking One-Night Stand', *Business Week,* **18**, (October), p. 12.

Lawler, E., S. Mohrman and G. Ledford (1992), *Employee Involvement and Total Quality Management: Practices and Results in Fortune 1000 Companies*, San Francisco: Jossey-Bass.

Madison, A. (1982), *Phases of Capitalist Development*, Oxford: Oxford University Press.

Mann, N.R. (1989), *The Keys to Excellence: The Story of the Deming Philosophy*, Los Angeles: Prestwick Books.

Matsushita, K. (1988), 'The Secret is Shared', *Manufacturing Engineering*, **100**, (2).

Miller, C. (1992), 'TQM's Value Criticised in New Report', *Marketing News*, (November), p. 1.

Miller, K.L., D. Woodruff and T. Peterson (1992), 'Japanese Drive to Cut Costs, *Business Week,* (December 21), pp. 34–9.

Mogab, J. and A. Bós (1992), 'Technological change: An institutionalist comparison of the continuous improvement and mass production firms', Paper presented to the Southwestern Economics meeting, Austin, Texas, March.

Muther, D. and L. Lytle (1992), 'Quality Education Requirements', in Ernst and Young Quality and Improvement Consulting Group, *Total Quality: A Manager's Guide for the 1990's*, London: Kogan Page Limited.

Myrdal, G. (1968), *Asian Drama*, New York: Penguin Books.

Nayak, P. and J. M. Ketteringham (1986), *Breakthroughs*, New York: Rawson.

New, C. (1988), 'U.K. Manufacturing: The Challenge of Transformation', (unpublished paper), Crafield School of Management.

Pascale, R.T. (1992), 'Zen and the Art of Management', in H.W. Lane and J.J. DiStefano (eds.), *International Management Behavior,* Boston: PWS-Kent Publishing Company.

Perkins, D. (1991), 'Economic Systems Reform in Developing Countries', in D. Perkins and M. Roemer (eds.), *Reforming Economic Systems in Developing Countries*, Cambridge: Harvard University Press.

Piccinini, V. (1990), 'L'Industrie de la Chaussure Brésilienne Face aux Mutations Internationales: Stratégies et Politique du Personnel des Enterprises de la Région de "Vales dos Sinos"', Unpublished Ph.D.Thesis, University of Grenoble.

Porter, M. (1990), *The Competitive Advantage of Nations*, New York: The Free Press.

Posthuma, A. C. (1993), 'Organizational Innovation in Zimbabwe: The Viability of Sustainable Change', *IDS Bulletin,* **24**, (2), pp. 10–18.

Ramirez, J.C. (1993), 'Recent Transformations in the Mexican Motor Industry', *IDS Bulletin,* **24**, (2), pp. 58–64.

Ray, S.M. (1992), 'Building World-Class Suppliers', in Ernst and Young Quality and Improvement Consulting Group, *Total Quality: A Manager's Guide for the 1990's*, London: Kogan Page Limited.

Reeve, J.M. (1991), 'Activity-Based Cost Systems for Functional Integration and Customer Value', in M.J. Stahl and G.M. Bounds (eds.), *Competing Globally Through Customer Value*, Westport, CT: Quorum Books.

Rodriguez, J.R. (1992), 'Total Productive Maintenance', in Ernst and Young Quality and Improvement Consulting Group, *Total Quality: A Manager's Guide for the 1990's*, London: Kogan Page Limited.

Ruas, R. (1989), 'Difusão de novas paradigmas da produção industrial: convergência e especifidades em dois segmentos industriais', Anais, Padroes Tecnológicos e Políticas de Gestão: Comparaçoes Internacionais, University of São Paulo, Brazil.

Ruas, R. (1993), 'Notes on the Implementation of Quality and Productivity Programmes in Sectors of Brazilian Industry', *IDS Bulletin,* **24**, (2), pp. 27–33.

Schonberger, R.J. (1982), *Japanese Manufactutring Techniques*, New York: The Free Press.

Schonberger, R.J. (1986), *World Class Manufacturing: The Lessons of Simplicity Applied*, New York: The Free Press.

Schramm, S. (1994), 'Beyond Firm Learning: The Emergence of a Concurrent Model of Technological Change', Unpublished doctoral dissertation, University of Tennessee, Knoxville.

Seckler, D. and K. Nobe (1983), 'The Management Factor in Developing Economies', *Issues in Third World Development*, Boulder: Westview Press.

Shaiken, H. and H. Browne (1991), 'Japanese Work Organization in Mexico', in G. Szekely (ed.), *Manufacturing Across Borders and Oceans: Japan, the United States, and Mexico*, San Diego: UCSD Center for U.S.–Mexican Studies.

Shingo, S. (1986), *Zero Quality Control*, Cambridge, MA: Productivity Press.

Sklair, L. (1990), *Assembling for Development: The Maquila Industry in Mexico and the United States*, Boston: Unwin Hyman.

Stahl, M.J. and G.M. Bounds (1991), 'Global Competition: The Need for Business and Educational Responses', in M.J. Stahl and G.M. Bounds (eds.), *Competing Globally Through Customer Value,* New York: Quorum Books.

Suzaki, K. (1987), *The New Manufacturing Challenge*, New York: The Free Press.

Takahashi, Y. and T. Osada (1990), *TPM: Total Productive Maintenance*, Tokyo: Asian Productivity Organization.

Trompenaars, F. (1993), *Riding the Waves of Culture*, London: The Economist Books Ltd.

UNIDO (United Nations Industrial Development Organization) (1979), *Conceptual and Policy Framework for Appropriate Industrial Technology: Monographs on Appropriate Industrial Technology, ID/232/1*, Vienna: UNIDO.

UNIDO (United Nations Industrial Development Organization) (1991), 'Training Industrial Managers in Least Developed Countries', Paper presented at the UNIDO Workshop held in Vienna, 19–23 August, ID/WG.515/6 (SPEC.), Austria.

UNIDO (United Nations Industrial Development Organization) (1993), *Industrial Management and Training in the United Republic of Tanzania: A Case Study of the Matsushita Electric Company (E.A.) Ltd.*, PPD.244 (SPEC.), Vienna: UNIDO.

Wadsworth, H.M., K.S. Stephens and G.A. Blanton (1986), *Modern Methods for Quality Control and Improvement*, New York: Wiley.

Walker, J.P. (1988), *A Disciplined Approach to Continuous Improvement*, Warren, OH: Packard Electric.

Walton, M. (1989), *The Deming Management Method*, London: Mercury Books.

Wilson, S. R. (1992), 'Continuous Improvement and the New Competition: The Case of U.S., European, and Japanese Firms in the Mexican Maquiladora Industry', Unpublished doctoral dissertation, The University of Tennessee, Knoxville.

Yoshida, K. (1989), 'Deming Management Philosophy: Does it work in the U.S. as well as in Japan?', *Columbia Journal of World Business*, **XXIV**, (3), pp. 10–17.

# Index